PRAISE FOR *INTENTIONAL CHURCHES*

"*Intentional Churches* is an invaluable resource that could single-handedly transform the impact of your church. Bart Rendel and Doug Parks bring years of hands-on experience, born in the trenches of ministry, to help leaders clarify their vision and align their passion with their practices. This is a book to read and reread with your team to increase your impact exponentially."

—JUD WILHITE, SENIOR PASTOR OF CENTRAL CHURCH; AUTHOR, *PURSUED*

"With lostness growing in North America, churches must become more effective than ever before at reaching their communities with the gospel. I believe as churches and individuals discover, pray for, and share the gospel with their ONE (as Bart and Doug describe in this book), people will meet the Lord, grow as disciples, and be deployed on mission around the world."

— KEVIN EZELL, PRESIDENT, NORTH AMERICAN MISSION
BOARD, SBC, ALPHARETTA, GEORGIA

"In our fast-changing world, nothing is more essential (or as challenging) as leading our teams with clarity, purpose, and focused goals. If you are looking to move your team from circular discussions into forward actions, ChurchOS is for you!"

—KADI COLE, LEADERSHIP CONSULTANT, EXECUTIVE COACH;
AUTHOR, *DEVELOPING FEMALE LEADERS*, WWW.KADICOLE.COM

"Any operating system is only as good as the character and experience behind the design of that system. Intentional Churches and its leaders embody not only high character and spiritual fervor in their mission, but have the depth of experience to bring practical and effective systems to life."

—BRAD LEEPER, PRINCIPAL, GENERIS

"Intentional Churches has been a great friend to the General Baptist denomination over the past several years. We are so excited about this book because finally the content we have learned at our conferences and workshops is available."

—CLINT COOK, PRESIDENT, THE GENERAL BAPTIST DENOMINATION

"Doug and Bart have worked with hundreds of churches, refining and implementing the principles that made the Great Commission so powerful in the first century. Those of us who have benefited from their expertise and experience have been asking them to put these principles in a book to make them more accessible. If you are a church leader, this book is a game changer for reaching your community."

—SHANE PHILIP, SENIOR PASTOR, THE CROSSING, LAS VEGAS, NEVADA

"If you are a leader with a vision, you need to read *Intentional Churches*. Bart and Doug have written a book and developed a system that will give you the pathway to reach your vision and beyond. I am convinced churches that engage with this process will experience exponential impact through a healthy team."

—GREG LIGON, CHIEF INNOVATION OFFICER, LEADERSHIP NETWORK

"*Intentional Churches* will challenge you and your team to make Luke 15 a driving force that aligns your church to reach more people for Christ."

—RON SYLVIA, LEAD PASTOR, CHURCH @ THE SPRING, OCALA, FLORIDA

"*Intentional Churches* takes you back to the purpose of the church. You will be challenged and encouraged to elevate the priority of reaching those far from God. If you love the gospel and people, then I guarantee these principles and stories will chart a course for you as a Christian leader."

—DAVE STONE, FORMER SENIOR PASTOR, SOUTHEAST
CHRISTIAN CHURCH, LOUISVILLE, KENTUCKY

"*Intentional Churches* provides the strategic tools, insights, and valuable action steps from practitioners who love the church and have been in the trenches. This book is a must-read and will be the book I give to my ministry friends this year."

—RICK RUSAW, GLOO EXECUTIVE; AUTHOR, *EXTERNALLY FOCUSED
CHURCH* AND *THE NEIGHBORING CHURCH*, LONGMONT, COLORADO

"If you are shopping for a book filled with cookie cutter quick fixes that promise to make your church grow overnight, then you have come to the wrong place. However, if you are looking for a strategic operating system that can guide you and your team through a clear and compelling process of discovering your church's unique contribution in fulfilling the Great Commission, this is the book for you."

—DR. TIM HARLOW, SENIOR PASTOR, PARKVIEW CHRISTIAN CHURCH,
ORLAND PARK, ILLINOIS; AUTHOR, *WHAT MADE JESUS MAD*

INTENTIONAL
CHURCHES

NEXT
LEADERSHIP NETWORK

INTENTIONAL CHURCHES

HOW IMPLEMENTING AN **OPERATING SYSTEM**
CLARIFIES VISION, IMPROVES DECISION MAKING, AND STIMULATES GROWTH

BART RENDEL & DOUG PARKS

THOMAS NELSON
Since 1798

Published in Nashville, Tennessee, by Thomas Nelson. Thomas Nelson is a registered trademark of HarperCollins Christian Publishing, Inc.

Thomas Nelson titles may be purchased in bulk for educational, business, fund-raising, or sales promotional use. For information, please e-mail SpecialMarkets@ThomasNelson.com.

Unless otherwise noted, Scripture quotations are taken from the Holy Bible, New Living Translation. © 1996, 2004, 2007, 2013, 2015 by Tyndale House Foundation. Used by permission of Tyndale House Publishers, Inc., Carol Stream, Illinois 60188. All rights reserved.

Scripture quotations marked ESV are from the ESV® Bible (The Holy Bible, English Standard Version®). Copyright © 2001 by Crossway, a publishing ministry of Good News Publishers. Used by permission. All rights reserved.

Scripture quotations marked KJV are from the King James Version. Public domain.

Scripture quotations marked THE MESSAGE are from *The Message*. Copyright © by Eugene H. Peterson 1993, 1994, 1995, 1996, 2000, 2001, 2002. Used by permission of NavPress. All rights reserved. Represented by Tyndale House Publishers, Inc.

Scripture quotations marked NIV are from the Holy Bible, New International Version®, NIV®. Copyright © 1973, 1978, 1984, 2011 by Biblica, Inc.® Used by permission of Zondervan. All rights reserved worldwide. www.Zondervan.com. The "NIV" and "New International Version" are trademarks registered in the United States Patent and Trademark Office by Biblica, Inc.®

Any Internet addresses, phone numbers, or company or product information printed in this book are offered as a resource and are not intended in any way to be or to imply an endorsement by Thomas Nelson, nor does Thomas Nelson vouch for the existence, content, or services of these sites, phone numbers, companies, or products beyond the life of this book.

Activation Dashboard, ChurchOS, ChurchOS Living Toolbox, Engagement Pathway, Great Commission Engine, Intentional Churches, Intentional Growth Planning, IGP, Priorities for Impact, Relational Reach Zone, Six Domains of Church, and the arrow logo are registered trademarks of Intentional Churches. Four Helpful Lists is used by permission from the Paterson Center, LLC.

ISBN 978–1–4002–1719–9 (eBook)
ISBN 978–1–4002–1718–2 (TP)

Library of Congress Control Number: 2019955115

Printed in the United States of America
HB 09.02.2022

About Leadership ✵ Network

Leadership Network fosters innovation movements that activate the church to greater impact. We help shape the conversations and practices of pacesetter churches in North America and around the world. The Leadership Network mind-set identifies church leaders with forward-thinking ideas—and helps them to catalyze those ideas, resulting in movements that shape the church.

Together with HarperCollins Christian Publishing, the biggest name in Christian books, the NEXT imprint of Leadership Network moves ideas to implementation for leaders to take their ideas to form, substance, and reality. Placed in the hands of other church leaders, that reality begins spreading from one leader to the next . . . and to the next . . . and to the next, where that idea begins to flourish into a full-grown movement that creates a real, tangible impact in the world around it.

NEXT: A Leadership Network Resource
committed to helping you grow your next idea.

leadnet.org/NEXT

CONTENTS

PHASE THREE: ORGANIZE

PHASE FOUR: ACTIVATE

To reach the ONE, in his name, only for his glory.

FOREWORD

I used to wear contact lenses. A while back, every time I put my contacts in my eyes before church services, everything would be fuzzy and blurry. I couldn't read my Bible or focus on my sermon notes. It was really frustrating and bothersome.

I don't know what prompted me to think about it, and I'm frankly embarrassed to admit it, but one weekend before services the thought hit me, *I wonder if somehow along the way I've gotten my lenses switched. Am I putting the one that goes in my left eye into my right eye and the one that goes in my right eye into my left eye?* So, I switched lenses. It was amazing how much better I could see! Imagine that.

I think this is what happens in the story of every church over time—we get our lenses switched. We get fuzzy about God's purpose and mission. We become inwardly focused. We become exclusive, instead of inclusive of the people God loves and for whom Jesus died.

This book is for every church leader who wants to get their lenses in the correct eyes. This book is for leaders like me, who sometimes lose focus but genuinely believe that if our vision became clear again, our plateaued or dying church could get back on track. Leaders who want to activate the Great Commission of Jesus and truly make an impact, maybe even double impact in the years to come.

On October 1, 2008, I became the pastor of Eastside Christian Church. Eastside is a church that had meant much to my life as a twenty-year-old intern years earlier. For a long time, it was a dramatically growing and high impact church. However, in 2008, we found ourselves in the same position 80 percent of churches are today—plateaued and declining. Our weekend attendance was down by more than 30 percent and our average age was rising dramatically.

Our problem was not a lack of effort. We had thirty-two ministries to help adults spiritually grow that required lots of energy, sacrifice, money, and prayer from very committed people. The irony was that the kingdom of God wasn't actually growing or expanding. Our problem wasn't effort, it was a lack of focus and no clarity of vision.

Along the way we got connected to our friends at Intentional Churches: Bart Rendel, Doug Parks, and their team. They helped us do less in order to do more and increase our intentionality when it comes to reaching and discipling more people. Their approach to helping churches dream new dreams and make great plans has not just helped us *double* the impact of our church, we have actually more than *quadrupled* the lives that are being impacted and discipled. My appreciation and respect for Bart and Doug could not be higher.

Here's what I believe: humble leaders who faithfully and prayerfully practice the principles in this book will see multiplied impact. This is a thoughtful, focused, and workable approach. However, it won't happen apart from courageous leaders, diligent prayer, and a carefully crafted and executed strategy.

When I first came to Eastside one of our longtime elders pulled me aside. Jerry Lauer was a little over seventy at the time. He had been a part of Eastside for more than forty years and a leader who had "his lenses" in the right eyes. This humble and courageous leader knew that unless Eastside made some significant changes, it was only a matter of time before our church became another statistic of churches closing their doors. Jerry pulled me aside and said, "Gene, we've got to do something different. So, lead us. We will do this together. And don't worry about the people who don't like change. I'll take care of the old people." And he did!

I'm convinced every church needs humble and courageous leaders like Jerry Lauer. I will forever be grateful to him and many others who had the courage and humility to say, "Let's rethink the way we're doing church. Let's pray and believe God for great things. Let's reimagine, reboot, and reignite a movement of disciple making in our corner of God's kingdom."

If you're reading this book, you're probably a leader with Jerry's heart. You want to see more impact in Jesus' name and are ready to do what it takes. This is the system for you. God bless you on your journey into ChurchOS.

GENE APPEL, SENIOR PASTOR
EASTSIDE CHRISTIAN CHURCH
ANAHEIM, CALIFORNIA

PREFACE

This is a trustworthy saying: "If someone aspires to be a church leader, he desires an honorable position."

—1 TIMOTHY 3:1

Your authors are addicts. Yes, it's true. We are addicted to the local church and its leaders. We can't get enough. We love the church in all its beauty and messiness. We love its glory, its challenges, and its infinite potential. It is our holy obsession, and we've committed our lives to serving the local church because it is God's chosen means of eternal impact in the world. It has forever changed our lives and our families.

Maybe you are an addict too. We assume you are a pastor, work with pastors, or know a pastor on some level. We also assume you love what you do even when what you do is hard or frustrating. In fact, maybe you're picking up this book and hoping to unlock some principle or learn about a system that has changed lives. Or maybe you just want to reignite your passion for the local church you serve. We hope all those things happen in the following pages.

My (Doug) life was changed forever through the impact of a local church youth pastor. He invited me into relationship with him and invested in my life through his ministry. My youth pastor gave me a vision for life in Christ and a place to call home. I entered ministry because of this vision and new identity and ended up in ministry at Canyon Ridge Christian Church in Las Vegas, Nevada (of all places!). My ministry in Las Vegas spanned seventeen years on the leadership team at The Ridge. Canyon Ridge shared my love and passion for the life-changing work of the local church.

I'm (Bart) a pastor's kid and the product of the local church. My mother and father planted two very successful churches. It was in these churches that I cut my teeth on the faith and grew a passion for ministry. I couldn't envision my gifting being used in the church, but God knew it could. I committed my life to church leadership late in high school, went to college, and ended up serving in two great ministries. The latter put me in Las Vegas, serving on the leadership team at Central Church. At Central, I saw courageous leadership, a systematic approach, and the power of patient improvement.

Together, our dream is to see a movement of Intentional Churches reaching and growing people like never before. We believe the movement is in its early stages. Here's what it means to be an Intentional Church and the twenty-one benchmarks against which these churches are measuring themselves:

- Mission is the Great Commission—nothing more, nothing less.
- Vision for double impact is stated and clear in timing and scope.
- Evaluation standards are clear and objective.
- Truth is spoken in the name of the mission—to the last 10 percent.
- Biblical fundamentals of Great Commission execution are known.
- Priorities are set and reviewed often—there are no sacred cows.

- Evangelistic growth is central to vision and planning.
- Connecting the lost to the church, Christ, and others is effective.
- Leadership dashboards are defined and reviewed regularly.
- Strategic activity is blended well with day-to-day activity.
- Structure and roles are defined for today and the future.
- Meetings are efficient and effective.
- Common language is defined and used.
- Routine planning is common to everyone.
- Champions for planning and accountability are established.
- Silver-bullet and quick-fix thinking are closely monitored.
- Governance and decision-making are growth oriented.
- Generosity and giving always have an active plan.
- Leadership development always has an active plan.
- Prayer always has an active plan.
- Church multiplication is a conviction.

This book is going to introduce you to the way to become an Intentional Church. If you apply what you learn here, you will begin this journey.

The book doesn't come from the realm of theory alone; it also comes from experience. We have dedicated ourselves to creating this movement. We began this work more than a decade ago and formed Intentional Churches (IC) for this sole purpose. The movement needed a common platform, so we created Intentional Growth Planning and ChurchOS—the fundamentals of which are described and defined in this book and are core to every Intentional Church.

Today, we continue to learn and build out the system alongside a team of trained coach-practitioners who use our system and help to train other leaders. We have committed to building IC with active and deeply experienced ministry practitioners. We have thousands of years of church leadership experience on our team, and this deep well of wisdom has greatly shaped ChurchOS.

This team has worked with more than three hundred churches of all backgrounds, types, and sizes to implement ChurchOS. Among them are brand-new church plants and two-hundred-year-old churches as well as churches ranging from twenty-five to twenty-five thousand in attendance. We have had the privilege of serving some of the fastest-growing churches in the United States. (Our churches have repeatedly been featured in the Outreach 100.) We have also had the honor of working with many churches and church leaders who are just as committed but may not be as well known. In each case, we used the same process and conversations outlined in this book. We have learned so much from this wonderful group of churches and leaders.

Within the pages of this book, we are going to walk you through ChurchOS, an operating system for an Intentional Church. It's going to be a comprehensive journey. We will lay out the foundations and principles that lie beneath the system. We will teach you how to objectify how you lead your church in a way that allows your team to have honest conversations unlinked from personal preferences. We will then show you the key repeatable, strategic conversation every gospel-centered church should be having with practical applications. And in the end we will pull it all together and make it come alive as an operating system with many examples and real-world applications. We want to help you go from frustrated to flourishing, not just growing in number but growing in kingdom impact.

We can't wait to tell you some of the compelling success stories of pastors and church leadership teams who are energized and gaining momentum. These churches are growing at an average rate of 15 percent in worship attendance and seeing God move in miraculous ways. They are growing not just by adding more programs or chasing fads but by systematically making more and better disciples. The leaders are clear and courageous and taking kingdom ground in his name and for his glory.

It's also important to realize what's not in this book. It is not a traditional strategic-planning manual where we walk you through the development of a vision, mission, values, and strategies for church. Others have gone before us and introduced strategic planning and great leadership methods to the church. We have learned from Donald McGavran, Charles and Win Arn, Aubrey Malphurs, Gary McIntosh, Joe Ellis, Will Mancini, Thom Rainer, Andy Stanley, Rick Warren, Eric Geiger, Tom Paterson, and more. You will see their insights and wisdom embedded in ChurchOS; however, ChurchOS is a unique strategic system that is comprehensive, with biblical fundamentals built into it.

One of the assumptions is related to the mission of the church. We believe the mission of the local church is summarized in Christ's Great Commission from Matthew 28:19–20. Based on this mission, we believe every church is called and commanded to *go* and *grow* its kingdom impact in his name. We call this command Great Commission *activation*.

Christ called us to go to the world, preach the gospel, baptize the uninitiated, and teach them to obey the very same thing we have been taught. In essence, this command pivots the followers from selfish living to being on Christ's mission both as individuals and members of the greater body of Christ. It's a mission that leads to ever-increasing impact and ongoing activation: making more and better disciples.

For this reason, you won't find us spending extensive time on developing mission statements—you can restate the Great Commission in any words that make sense for you so long as they align with Christ's call and command. Instead, you will find us teaching you how to have courageous conversations about today's battles, tomorrow's challenges, and the future's vision.

The local church is God's plan for the world. That plan has incredible implications. Do you realize that what happens each week in your church has eternal impact? Your own church's history, whether short or long, can be traced to the church that Jesus established while here on earth. The apostle Paul told us in Ephesians 3:10–11 that God intended an eternal purpose through the church. What you do matters.

We want you to know up front that ChurchOS is an evangelistically centered system. We are going to write a lot about some concepts we've coined, namely, the ONE and ONE-awareness. In fact, the whole system is centered on these concepts. We've asked many teams, "If you could double your ministry's impact by recruiting church members from another church down the street or taking more unsaved people to heaven, which would you choose?" The answer is obvious! You will see us bring this into focus again and again throughout this book.

We suspect that some parts of the book will confirm what you've already been thinking or possibly even trying. Other parts could lead to a revelation. We are praying for both confirmation and revelation and ultimately insight that will lead to courageous decisions, deep confidence that eradicates fear, and a clear plan to accomplish Christ's mission.

One final word: As the leader, Great Commission activation has *everything* to do with you and it has *nothing* to do with you at the same time! Our opportunity is to partner at the Lord's invitation. We are stewards of his church in this season. Your church has infinite power because of the gospel and the power of the Holy Spirit. The big question, and maybe the only one, is this: "Lord, what would you have us do in the next season to release the power of your gospel through our church?" When this power is released, amazing miracles happen, not of our power, but only his. And we will only know in heaven the eternal ripples of the impact made through our churches for his glory alone.

We have prayed for our intersection. Let's get started!

INTRODUCTION

God's purpose in all this was to use the church to display
his wisdom in its rich variety to all the unseen rulers and
authorities in the heavenly places. This was his eternal plan,
which he carried out through Christ Jesus our Lord.

—EPHESIANS 3:10–11

The local church is a miracle. It's a divine strategy that in human terms simply doesn't make sense. Why would the almighty God of the universe bring his Son to earth and then leave it up to us to make sure everyone hears the good news of Christ? Was this his chosen strategy? Really? He put the greatest message to be told in our feeble hands, and immediately trouble broke out.

The early church began with a promise of power as the Holy Spirit came upon them on the day of pentecost. Right away it was evident this was something special. Peter, John, and the rest of the apostles spoke boldly about Jesus, even in the face of opposition. Miracles were common and generosity was the standard. The city of Jerusalem was transformed, and thousands were being saved!

It wasn't long until the gospel spread, but problems reared their heads. The Greek Christians were being overlooked in the ministry to widows. The Jewish Christians were upset with the Gentiles' refusal to follow their customs. Even Paul, the first great missionary and church planter, had his fair share of conflicts with Peter, John Mark, and even his best friend, Barnabas. As powerful as the early church was, they had their share of problems.

But God didn't alter his plan. This seemingly flawed strategy has a divine purpose we will only fully understand in heaven. His plan has endured for over two thousand years and is still in play today.

Our first question in heaven will be, "Why did you entrust such an audacious plan to such imperfect people?" Maybe it was to put us in a place of utter dependency on him and the Holy Spirit. Maybe it was so the glory for our kingdom victories could only go to him. Who knows? What we do know is that he has promised to be with us in the execution of his mission, the Great Commission. And we know for sure we have a part to play in this mission on earth. What a privilege it is to lead his miraculous church.

THE CHALLENGE

It's a wonderful time to be a leader. We are more resourced than ever, with thousands of articles, books, blogs, podcasts, ideas, and strategies at our fingertips. We are living in a season when we have learned what works and what doesn't from the many who have gone before us. We stand on the shoulders of those who taught us how to hold great weekend experiences, plant effective churches, make disciples, create clear vision, be great neighbors, and serve our communities. But the church at large remains either stuck or retreating in terms of gospel impact.

Here are some troubling statistics. Ed Stetzer and our friends at Exponential and the North American Mission Board recently studied the landscape of the church in the United States.[1] There are more than 300,000 churches in America; however, it was determined that 80 percent are not growing or are in a state of decline, only 16 percent are growing numerically, a miniscule 4 percent are reproducing themselves through planting or multisite strategies, and effectively 0 percent are truly multiplying or creating spiritual movements. How can this be?

Since 2016 more churches are planted per year than are closing for the first time in many decades, but not by much. About 3,750 churches will close their doors this year and about 4,000 churches will be planted; however, only 60 percent of those planted are expected to survive beyond five years. In the next fifty years, analysts say 175,000 churches will fail.[2] That's more than half! This is a multifaceted challenge, and we need a God-born breakthrough to stem this tide.

We all sense something must change. This conviction has led to extraordinary efforts to develop countless topical solutions. The good-willed efforts of very smart leaders, combined with today's digital distribution infrastructure, have led to the mass availability of church leadership resources on more topics than ever, but with little mass affect. We believe the core of the challenge is the lack of a master rubric or set of church leadership filters through which these resources can be sorted, chosen, and implemented.

The problem doesn't lie in the brilliance of the resources. In this tremendously resourced season of church leadership, is it possible we have a problem born out of conviction? Could it be that in order to reach the lost and grow his people—a burden every good leader feels—we have potentially chased solutions and forgotten the basics? We all have a sense of urgency and wake up each morning with a heavy call upon us. Have we opted for speed because of this conviction? If so, you could see where this would lead us toward impetuous leadership and limited, even declining, success.

It goes something like this. We go to a conference, read a book or blog, or hear something from a pastor friend, and with a sense of urgency born from deep conviction, we quickly swap our current strategy for a new solution, hoping it will work. It doesn't matter if the prior solution is only a few weeks underway, time is of the essence. Eternity is at stake. We should try anything that might work! Sometimes it does, but most times it doesn't. When it does, we probably can't tell you why it worked all that well. But eventually it will quit working and the silver-bullet search will resume, potentially wasting precious time and resources.

If we are going to change the declining and limited impact of the church in North America (and possibly beyond), we need a robust and comprehensive solution that cuts through silver-bullet thinking in this overinformed era. It means declaring war on old paradigms and becoming proactive in sorting through a plethora of today's well-meaning but limited topical solutions. A transcendent solution needs to be broadly applicable. It must help churches of all types to get back to the basics.

Declining churches must catch a vision for turnaround and be equipped with the tools and coaching to make it happen. Plateaued churches must grow in conviction that their best days are ahead. Growing churches and new church plants must never be content with the status quo, because every church was called to *go* and *grow* by Christ. We need an army of Intentional Churches. Great courage and clarity are required, and together we can see a new day emerge.

It is time for double impact! We will talk about impact in more detail, but in short, kingdom impact is the ripple effect that only life change in Christ can bring. It's about transformation. Transformation of lives, communities, families, and generations through the power of the gospel. That impact takes many forms. And yes, we can measure it, meaning we should be counting how many people are connected to our church families, giving and serving, but we should be measuring much more. We will talk more extensively about this as we go.

A UNIFYING THEORY

In the early 1900s, Albert Einstein developed the theory of relativity. For now, it remains the best explanation of how the universe works when it comes to energy, expansion, and masses. It's summarized in a formula: $E = mc^2$. Einstein wasn't inventing the universe or even defining it all that much—he was interpreting its dynamics. But in doing so, Einstein unlocked everything from space travel to quantum physics. Believe it or not, your life is deeply impacted every day by Einstein's work. You don't have to create something new to have lasting impact. You only need to interpret the dynamics and learn how they fundamentally apply to life.

So how did God design the church? Could there be a unified theory that would help us all understand how to lead our churches? How to be more intentional? If so, we could all get back to basics and understand God's intent for the local church. We could also build systems and innovations based on this fundamental truth, a rubric through which our thinking and choices could be filtered.

We submit there are scriptural foundations that point us to a unifying theory for church leadership and growth. And we have built an operating system on these foundational truths any church can use day after day. We call it ChurchOS.

AN OPERATING SYSTEM

We are all familiar with operating systems. Every computer you own, whether it's a laptop or a desktop, has a program that determines how you interface with it and how productive it can be. About every other month, it seems, our smartphones ask us to run an update to ensure they still work properly. What do these digital tools all have in common? There's a system that makes the hardware and software work in a way that creates incredible efficiency and productivity. It's called an operating system (OS). An operating system is the filter through which inputs and outputs are processed. It is the foundation upon which software and applications run.

That's what a ChurchOS is too. It's a comprehensive set of

leadership tools that have broad applications built on unifying biblical foundations. It's a system that makes the hardware (the gospel, people, buildings, and finances) and the software (today's and tomorrow's ministry strategies and solutions) work together incredibly well today and tomorrow. It's a system that eliminates the search for the next silver-bullet strategy.

We are going to unpack the fundamentals and principles of the ChurchOS platform in a way you can immediately apply to your church. It's simple, repeatable, and on the way to creating a movement of like-minded and effective churches.

FOUNDATIONS: We will start by taking you through the principles for a new day in church leadership. These principles are in use by some leaders, but we have a feeling a few of them will be inspiring and challenging for you. We will also lay out the basic constructs on which the ChurchOS is built. It's an important section you won't want to skip.

DISCOVERY: We will describe our primary tools for team-based self-discovery on the Six Domains of Church. We have found these tools to be clarifying. They simplify the local church and your role in leading it. They create common paradigms and a language you can customize as needed.

DESIGN: In this section we will talk about the key design tools for every church. Who are you going to reach? How will you connect them to you and Christ? What is your vision for the future? These are key ministry design questions. We will address these key questions and give you the practical tools for application to your church and your team.

ORGANIZE: Great discovery and design would be fruitless if we didn't draw conclusions and organize for action. Organizing for action can be tough in the church because the day-to-day rhythm and reality of church is so nonstop demanding. There is a "today" and a "tomorrow" reality to church leadership that must be constantly managed, and we will address both.

ACTIVATE: To activate the Great Commission (the making of more and better disciples) you must develop great routines, a means of measuring and monitoring progress, and disciplines for execution. We will give you the tools to develop great habits and routines that lead to greater kingdom impact.

ARCHITECTS WITH A PURPOSE

How is all this talk about operating systems, strategic conversations, double impact, and evaluation sitting with you as a church leader? Some of you love this side of ministry leadership. You are wired for maps, models, and modes of ministry, and all of this arouses your interest. That's definitely me (Bart). The local church has been integral to my life for as long as I can remember, so much so that there is little to no distinction between my chosen vocation and the very essence of who I am. I was raised in the home of a pastor and a mother who simply loved ministry—all of it. Late in high school I heard the Lord whisper there was no greater life commitment I could make than to use my skills and unique gifts to serve his church.

The problem, however, was the lack of clarity about what form this would take. I had an affinity for math, design, and business. I'm not wired like my gifted pastor-preacher-evangelist father. This was confusing to a degree. Clarity came when I traveled with my father and his team to a Willow Creek Community Church leadership conference. My life and vision for ministry were altered forever. Two things struck me profoundly: (1) the church's priority is the reaching of the lost and (2) there are strategies to be discerned and implemented that can make us more effective at reaching the lost. I could finally see my role emerging. Back in high school, I started a folder after my visit to Willow Creek that remains in my files today. It is labeled "Maps, Models, and Modes of Ministry." For real. I still have it. I was on the hunt for the perfect model. After decades in ministry, I realize there is such a thing, but it's more fundamental and scriptural than I knew back then.

I (Doug) didn't grow up in the church like Bart. I'm a pastor with a past. The trajectory of my life today is radically different than where it could have been, and this is because of the power of Christ through other people. It is why I love Jesus and his church deeply. God transformed my life through people who poured into me—from my youth pastor in high school, to deep friendships in college, and through one of my first bosses at Chick-fil-A.

God used friends from that rich community in college to call me into church planting in Las Vegas. My background and the culture in Vegas have been a good match. You see, in Vegas there is no pretense. People will come right up to you and tell you about getting drunk the night before, even at church in conversation with their pastors. While that might be shocking to some leaders, because of my family history, I could identify with the realities of that messy life. It was also the vulnerability and authenticity I needed. That church plant, Canyon Ridge Church, grew rapidly and today averages more than seven thousand in weekend attendance. The tools and mentors God gave me at Chick-fil-A—facilitating meetings, equipping individuals well, and building good teams—have all been utilized. I love being an architect for God's kingdom purposes and seeing personal transformation.

You might be a leader like Bart's father—you're an evangelist, a preacher, or possibly a worship leader. You are wired to share the gospel through teaching or storytelling, worship or other forms of expression. You want to help people connect to God's truth and deepen their relationship with him. All this talk of operating systems and evaluations might seem cumbersome or like a foreign language. Many of us in ministry have seminary degrees but not organizational leadership training. Let's be honest, your executive pastor, church administrator, or an elder might have handed you this book!

We want you to trust us. At the heart of ChurchOS is the Great Commission. If someone handed you this book, it's likely they want to bring their gifts and skills to the grand adventure and miracle called the church. No matter what position you have or how you are wired, the alignment and direction you have to gain as a God-ordained team and leader will far outweigh your personal feelings and style. Every path we hope to lead you down is ultimately about partnering with God and his power to make more and better disciples for his glory.

STEWARDS ON A MISSION

We are all stewards of his church in this season. And with his help, we will hand it to the next generation in great shape. That is our calling: to take the leadership of his bride seriously but hold it loosely so he can do what he wants with and through us. We desperately want to see the footprint of kingdom impact expand through our churches. We want to see more people in heaven, relationships made whole, and the trajectory of generations and even nations radically altered for good.

We hope in these pages your passion for the church will be ignited and fueled. Your church is an outpost of the gospel in your neck of the woods. Your church is likely filled with good people who love and follow Jesus. We need your church, the church next door, and the church across town (including the missional church, the attractional church, the small church, the declining church, the emerging church, and the megachurch) to all dream and plan for double impact in his name.

It's been said the church is the hope of the world, but we firmly believe the good news of Jesus is actually the hope of the world. The church is his chosen, radical, providential means of communicating the good news to the world. It's a miracle. So how can we do better? How can we help to turn the tide and see his church truly prevail in the coming years and generations?

This has been our quest and calling, and we are thankful you are joining us. We believe that by going back to basics, building on a biblical unifying theory, and putting our churches on a common operating system, we can eliminate fear and create a movement of evangelistically focused, disciple-making churches like never before.

Intentional Churches are led by Intentional Leaders. Before we dive into the specifics of Intentional Growth Planning and ChurchOS, let's start with you as a leader. A new day requires a new kind of leader.

FOUNDATIONS

ONE

THE INTENTIONAL LEADER

It's important that a church leader, responsible for the affairs in God's house, be looked up to—not pushy, not short-tempered, not a drunk, not a bully, not money-hungry. He must welcome people, be helpful, wise, fair, reverent, have a good grip on himself, and have a good grip on the Message, knowing how to use the truth to either spur people on in knowledge or stop them in their tracks if they oppose it.

—TITUS 1:7–9 THE MESSAGE

There's a pastor in your hometown. Let's call him Jim. He's not new to this pastoring thing. He's been the lead pastor of his church for a while now, maybe ten years. As a committed leader, he's no stranger to the latest and greatest leadership models. He's heard them all and tried enough of them. Jim found some success in going to a conference now and then, reading a book, or studying another church's strategy.

Jim is excited about the local church, fully committed, even if he's busy most days. He tries his best to balance family time with work commitments. There's the new building project the board keeps asking about. And the job of hiring a new NextGen pastor. His plate is pretty full.

Meanwhile, growth has stagnated. A few hundred show up each

week, but it's been that way for a while. Jim feels plateaued in his ministry and leadership. What should be a reason to celebrate is often the object of frustration and a reminder of what isn't working. He feels the pressure to move the church forward, reach more people in the community, and do it while not taking on a lot of new responsibilities. It's just that every time he tries something new, there's a little bit of success before things swing back to square one.

Sound familiar? Maybe you've had coffee with Pastor Jim and listened to his frustrations. Maybe you've served on his staff, scratching your head alongside him about why the church just feels stuck. You might be a volunteer on this team.

Or maybe Pastor Jim is you.

We understand. We see a lot of ourselves in Jim. Just like him, we are excited about the local church. And we know that young leaders think and behave differently than most. We've worked with churches that thrive and others that were just trying to survive. A shared reality to all of them is that everything rises and falls on leadership. We believe in a new approach to church leadership. This new approach will give you courage, confidence, and hope. The best days of your church are ahead of you!

ChurchOS is about clearing out the frustrations of the copy-and-paste mentality. It's designed to both create and support a leader who leads differently and courageously. Intentionally! It will push you to break away from the old habits and traditional approaches. When you see the pieces click together, we think you'll see the difference.

Before we dive into ChurchOS, we need to outline the characteristics of this new approach. Think of this as the end-user agreement. Without these in place, we cannot guarantee your success. We've outlined ten necessary commitments for you and your team. If you are going to lead your church into the future, you better get ready to be challenged on these new approaches.

This book is interactive. At the end of each section, grade yourself on how well you're doing in that area. Evaluate yourself from A to F.

It would be helpful to dedicate a separate journal to the work you will do relating to this book.

- **A** = acing it almost always
- **B** = somewhat true but you have room for improvement
- **C** = so-so leader on this one
- **D** = there is a lot of room before this is fully integrated
- **F** = failing for sure at this one

Now, no leader is perfect, but if you are consistently ignoring many of these commitments, you will find implementing ChurchOS a potential challenge. This might be a chapter you want to refer to down the road if you find yourself struggling.

LEADING WITH A TEAM

Without people to follow your vision, you aren't really leading, you're just going for a walk. It's imperative you don't take people for granted. Think of the team you lead. The people you lead are not just your staff, though they may be very important. They're also your church people. They are volunteers and key lay leaders who help you reach your weekly goals. They are also the people in the seats and those in your community not yet sitting there. In a way, you lead them all.

You are about to learn a way to mine the wisdom of a team, but it can't work unless you see the value of that team. It requires synergy on your part. Listening and responding to your team. You must be on the same page. There's nothing more frustrating than a team member who flies solo, including you.

An old approach was to send the senior leader to the mountaintop, like Moses, to hear from God and bring back the vision and instructions. This puts immense pressure on the senior leader and can breed a lack of confidence in the team. We firmly believe the senior leader must fully weigh into the vision and plan, but the team's wisdom must also be included.

A new approach is to level the playing field. Instead of the pastor out front alone, find your place as part of the team. Literally put yourself at the leadership table with the team. The church is often tempted to label one person as "God's man for the job." In practice, it's so much better when you all lead together instead of alone.

ChurchOS is designed for church leaders who lead with a team. In fact, it also facilitates it, as you will see in this book. You cannot successfully activate the Great Commission as a solo act. As you work through it, you'll see how it truly takes a team commitment. Pastors who lead with a team find it easiest to adapt along the way.

How are you doing as a leader who leads with a team? Give yourself a grade from A to F. My grade: _____

Consider using a separate journal to record your answers.

COMMON LANGUAGE

Have you ever noticed how many words have multiple meanings within the church world? Take the word *discipleship,* for instance. Ten people will give you as many different definitions. What about *core values*? For some it's about what we value most as a church. For others it's about setting standards for our behaviors and guardrails for our strategies. Even there, the nuances are so subtle, they're nearly indiscernible, but there is a difference.

Jesus was brilliant when it came to communication. When he used words like *kingdom*, his followers knew what he meant. When he taught crowds, he pulled words from everyday life. His message was clear and to the point, and his leadership showed it.

There are some big benefits to intentionally creating a common language for your team. Here are just a few:

SPEED: As you lead your team, it's vital you share a common language. It *creates momentum*. Instead of spending time explaining what you need from your people or cleaning up some miscommunication, you can quickly convey your vision and needs and get things done.

CULTURE: A common language *sustains good culture*. It's important to create a culture of effective ministry on your team. You want to celebrate wins and feel close as a team. What happens after you lay out values and strategy and then rely on each team member's interpretation to drive it? With a common language, you can be sure that culture grows deep, lasting roots.

EXPECTATIONS: A common language *cuts through misunderstanding*. When you rely on a common language, your people know what's expected. They assume the best of you as a leader and the best of each other. It can help lower the friction that occurs between people. Since you're speaking the same language, you can resolve misunderstandings quicker and without hard feelings.

One of the early wins of ChurchOS is the common language we promote. We will give you a package of concepts, words, and language. As you get accustomed to our lingo, you can adjust the language to what works best with your team, but pay attention to establishing labels and language as you go.

What's the level of the use of common language at your church currently? Give yourself a grade from A to F. My grade: _____

SYSTEMATIC APPROACH

Today's change leaders use systems. Some pastors are uncomfortable with that type of language. If you lean on a system, does that mean you're relying less on the Holy Spirit? Not necessarily. Look at the following example.

The apostle Paul was a master church planter. But as you read the account of his life and ministry, something obvious begins to emerge. In Acts 13, the Christians in Antioch were praying when the Holy Spirit spoke to them, telling them to enlist Paul to go and tell as many people as possible about Jesus.

The *challenge* was to go to towns and countries where the gospel had never been shared. The *goal* was to establish churches there. Paul became the first church planter of the early church. But how was he going to do it? There were no patterns to follow, no books to read, no conferences to attend. He came up with a strategy on his own through the wisdom of the Holy Spirit. And what developed was a system. He would first go to the Jews, preaching in their synagogues. If that didn't work, he would turn to the Gentiles. Once people received Christ, he would establish house churches under the leadership of local Christians before moving on to the next town. He did this over and over again, from Galatia to Ephesus to Athens to Thessalonica. And it worked!

After Paul's first missionary journey, his future trips followed that same pattern. Why? Because a repeatable system can predict success. He was able to survey the landscape upon arrival and implement quickly. That's what a system does for leaders who are willing to make changes. You can predict your level of success when you commit to a system.

A system follows a logical sequence of events. It gives you a list of points to fire in sequence that build on the prior one. When you implement a good system, there are certain built-in deliverables.

SUSTAINABILITY: You are learning a system that can be used over time by multiple users. Throughout staff turnover, organizational restructures, building programs, and ministry overhauls, the power of a system is its ability to hold up under rapid change. That sustainability allows you to focus on the important aspects of ministry without worrying about shifting systems and language every few months or years.

EFFICIENCY: The simple user interface makes it quick to implement.

Getting in and out at the beginning of your workflow is essential to staying on top of the things that really matter. A system with built-in efficiency will allow you to stay on task longer.

SCALE: This is a must for the long-term effects of any system. Paul knew this. Whether it was a large metropolis or a small village, he adapted his system to the changing landscape. ChurchOS functions in smaller churches, growing churches, larger churches, you name it. The system is not held back by the size of the staff, the size of the building, or whether the church is multisite or not. As you grow, it grows with you.

COLLABORATION: Any good system allows for collaboration. There is a user group that can learn from one another. When you are using a common language and approach, collaboration becomes a natural by-product. A hallmark of today's leader is one who creates, leans into, and allows for collaboration. We are better together in church leadership.

We believe in the ChurchOS system. This doesn't mean it replaces the need for the Spirit's direction. In Acts 13, at the beginning of Paul's ministry, it was an act of the Holy Spirit that spurred him to engage in a system. The reason he relied on that system so often is because it came from an earnest relationship with the living God. As you'll see later, that's the same passion he placed in us.

How are you currently employing systems? Give yourself a grade from A to F. My grade: _____

OBJECTIVE EVALUATION

Great change leaders must be willing to evaluate objectively. While that sounds like a no-brainer, often the church's evaluation process includes subjective criteria. When we're afraid to sacrifice a sacred cow or upset a certain sector, our evaluation ends up thin and ineffective.

What do you do when your car isn't running right? You take it to the shop. Do you hope they give it a quick look, tell you it sounds fine, and send you on your way? Or would you rather they pop the hood and look around, take it to the back, put it up on the rack, and look into every system and part? Of course you're going to want them to do as thorough a job as they can on your car. Otherwise, they may not find out what's wrong with it.

Being a good steward does not mean pampering. It means making tough decisions based on objective analysis. Until you can objectify evaluation, each change will be stilted at best and counterproductive at worst. To keep everyone happy, you'll shade every evaluation to make it look like everything is rosy. We'll talk more about this soon.

We love the church! As Christ's bride, we are committed to doing whatever it takes to ensure her health. That means we take an objective view of it, even while we are passionate about each member. We can take it seriously while holding it loosely.

ChurchOS is a way to pop the hood of your church, so to speak, and look at it objectively. It's about getting into every part and seeing what's running right, what needs attention, and maybe what needs to go. It's serious business, but it's God's business.

Approaching your church with an objective viewpoint is difficult. We will provide you with some paradigms that will help, but it won't make it any easier. It's tough to look at the things that have gone wrong, often for years, and not flinch. But good leaders are willing to listen to problems and make needed changes.

One word of advice: toughen your skin. Get ready to hear some things you don't want to hear. Be prepared to be challenged to take actions you never thought you'd have to take. There is a ministry you may have to stop, a position you may need to cut, a program that has run its course, a paradigm that is holding you back. Are you and your team ready?

How are you doing at objective evaluation? Give yourself a grade from A to F. My grade: _____

COMPLETE HONESTY

Our churches are full of grace, but they are also full of truth. Unfortunately, our evaluations and plans are sometimes characterized by incomplete honesty. It's not that we don't want to be completely honest, but we are grace filled and sometimes reluctant to speak the full truth because of this grace. But there is that final bit, the last 10 percent that goes uncovered. If you don't find it, it can limit your gospel impact.

We're sure you've heard or quoted Numbers 32:23: "But if you fail to do this, you will be sinning against the LORD; and you may be sure that your sin will find you out" (NIV).

There is a saying, made popular by Tom Paterson, that borrows from that thought: "Find a truth before it finds you."[1] In other words, there are aspects of your character, your framework, your ministry that may be undermining you. It is difficult to face these hard truths. But ignoring them won't make them go away. In fact, they will fester in the darkness.

Trust us, the last 10 percent of truth is your breakthrough! Satan wants to use it to undermine the great kingdom plans for your church. But you can turn that around and use it as the launching pad for something great. King David's weakness was the cause of great damage in his life. But once he faced the truth and repented his sins, he saw some of the greatest growth possible. His life and leadership were forever changed.

We worked with a team in Cincinnati that had seen some incredible success over the years. They were a church of over a thousand people but in dire straits under the surface. The team was intimidated, overworked, and interpersonally stuck. The water-cooler conversations were out of control. After our first day of working together, the senior pastor felt led by the Spirit to ask his team to open up and be honest about his leadership and the team's dynamics. Once the ice broke the next morning, the team began to share the intimidation they had felt under his leadership, giving specific examples. This humility and honest moment led to an interpersonal revolution that completely changed the culture of the team. They were finally ready to grow.

So push for the last 10 percent of truth. It affects your gospel impact! You must do so for the sake of the gospel! Systems that are implemented and run properly will shine a light on the things you thought weren't a problem, things you mistakenly assumed could be overlooked, or things you've been hiding from yourself. Leaders committed to change will embrace that truth, no matter how difficult it is.

How willing are you to encourage complete truth, especially about your church? Give yourself a grade from A to F. My grade: _____

SMART BULLETS, NOT SILVER BULLETS

The cure-all. The golden ticket. The silver bullet. That's what we're all hoping for. Imagine if we could give you one thing that would guarantee success no matter what. You could fire it up and let it run, knowing all your problems would be fixed. How much would you pay for it? How far would you go to get it? What would you be willing to lose to ensure that success?

Unfortunately, there are no silver bullets, but sadly, too many of us are waiting for one. We spend too many hours and too much money searching for it. Just because it worked for someone else doesn't mean it will for you. Your church is uniquely yours. To adopt what another church has had success with may give you quick, easy results. But it will often have a short lifespan and only brief growth. Great change leaders need to be looking for smart bullets, not silver bullets.

By objectifying your evaluation, you can make smarter choices. Instead of firing off a fix-all, use common filters and paradigms to make your ministry strategies make sense. Soon you will learn more about the Great Commission Engine, which will help you to streamline the necessary decisions. We don't fix everything magically. Instead, we help you understand how church works and focus your efforts in the right direction.

Nothing is sacred in ChurchOS. We only implement things so long as they work. That requires testing and retesting at every level. We pass every new idea through a filter. Rather than doing things and hoping for a beneficial outcome, we let the filters tell us if they are working right or not.

One pastor we worked with in the Midwest kept spinning his wheels as his church stagnated. He used the same cut-and-paste mentality that so many pastors do. These strategies gave him short bursts of success, but he quickly plateaued. His confidence was eroding along with his team's. The church was able to maintain an attendance of around a thousand, but there was always a ceiling. He was stuck. Every silver bullet he tried eventually misfired.

Coming alongside this pastor, we helped him to see how smart-bullet thinking is more advantageous. Through honest evaluation, we showed him that just copying the church down the street, across the state, or on the other side of the country was keeping him stuck. Relying on a system, rather than cloning a strategy, made all the difference.

Are you looking for silver bullets or smart bullets? Give yourself a grade from A to F. My grade: _____

ZERO-SUM LEADERSHIP

In game theory, a zero-sum means not everyone can win, there must be a winner and a loser. But within business models, the zero-sum view is an application of an obvious and honest assessment of your resources. It allows for making the right decisions at all times.

Great change leaders must take on a zero-sum mentality when it comes to the church. You have a finite amount of resources, including time and money. You are forced to work within those limits or suffer harm. When you stick to a conviction about a zero-sum strategy, you are not limiting God; you are simply acknowledging your own limitations.

Another way to look at it is by assessing your priorities. There is no innocent yes. When you say yes to something, you are saying no to something else. You don't have the money, the time, or the personnel to do everything. But as we meet with churches, we find that most think they can. So they stretch themselves too thin and end up overextended.

We could sit with you and evaluate every aspect of your church life. We could map it out based on its effectiveness, its drain on resources, and its ability to connect with your current vision. Chances are we would find that one-third of your projects need to be cut immediately. Without a zero-sum mind-set, you may never have the courage to make those difficult choices.

When you see your resources in a zero-sum context, the questions will be, "What *must* we do?" and "What is *best* to do?" not "What *can* we do?" or "What do we *want* to do?" That conviction will not only drive better decision-making, it will bring you to a point of decision. Once you decide to make the investment, you have to be honest with yourself. Where will the commitment in resources come from?

How are you handling the zero-sum of your resources? Give yourself a grade from A to F. My grade: _____

PRIORITIES, FOCUS, AND FOLLOW-THROUGH

There is no off-season in the church. It's a constant fifty-two-week rhythm. That can seem daunting to anyone, but great change leaders will embrace that pace by prioritizing, focusing, and following through. The ChurchOS system requires that type of attention and commitment.

To fully commit means you place a high priority on your work. You assign the task of running ChurchOS to one of your most passionate and competent staff members. You make sure all the other staff are bought in as well. It also means you focus. As you read through the different aspects of the interface, you'll get a picture of why this is so vital to success. But when you commit, the system that emerges will be worth it. Finally, you must follow through on your commitments.

Make sure you open proper channels for feedback and ensure all systems are running smoothly as often as possible.

That feels like a lot! But the payoff in increased Great Commission activation and impact is worth the price. Too often we sacrifice today's energy for tomorrow's energy. We believe if we can find the right cure, we will ultimately have enough focus or power to get over the hump. Or we believe spinning our wheels on the current system is good enough and will eventually catch on. But the truth is that you need to commit today's energy to a system that will bring you tomorrow's solutions.

The reason so many of us settle for short-term growth is that we lack patience. The world is full of get-rich-quick schemes that go nowhere, but the long haul has produced success after success. Jeff Bezos is arguably the most successful entrepreneur in America, launching an online business from his own garage. He committed energy and made it happen, often referred to as a "ten-year overnight success."[2]

Great ideas take time to take root. Are you willing to put in the effort? There's a lot of fun in starting something, but once the work begins, the excitement tends to fade. We tend to look for that same feeling when that something is no longer new. But there is great joy and satisfaction in completing things. Think of the celebrations you'll have when you commit to it and see it to the very end!

How are you doing with prioritization and focus? Give yourself a grade from A to F. My grade: _____

POWERFUL HABITS AND ROUTINES

Look on your bookshelf and you might find a book on habits. There are many currently available on the power of harnessing habits. Great change leaders must develop great habits. When we think of habits, we often think of ditching an old one. But when used positively, habits have a powerful, tremendous impact.

The first step in harnessing the power of habits is to think of the church you want your church to become. That requires goal setting and vision casting. Once you have that idea in focus, reverse engineer it by thinking of the habits you need to have in place to make it a reality. Go through your day. At a church that is meeting its goals, what do staff meetings look like? How do people organize their day? What are you prioritizing?

Now that you have that list in mind, get to work on developing them now. When you bake a cake, you don't start with the finished product. You gather the ingredients and follow the steps. What starts as some flour, eggs, and sugar will become the dessert you're hoping for. Healthy habits give you the ability to stick to the recipe. We will show you built-in mechanisms and defined habits.

Repetition is the key to mastery. Once you start those habits, continually refine them and repeat them. It's a lot like a workout program. You don't start a program and become an overnight bodybuilder. It takes patience and commitment. But any routine you stick to can produce results.

We jokingly say that ChurchOS is like P90X for a church leadership team! Built into the process are habits that can produce the results you're aiming for. But it requires repetition. Instead of just turning it on and letting it run, you must engage the system with routines.

We will walk you through these routines in the coming chapters, but it's important to understand now that any commitment you make must be backed up with the habits you'll be developing.

How are you doing with building positive habits and sticking with them? Give yourself a grade from A to F. My grade: _____

CONSTANT IMPROVEMENT

ChurchOS requires certain commitments from top to bottom. On all levels, your staff needs to be engaged and involved. If you've heard of the kaizen principle, you'll understand this.

American business executives were perplexed at how well Japanese businesses were run. They wanted to replicate their successes, so they analyzed some of the top companies, from Toyota to Sony. What they found was a business model not found in the West, one built on a discipline that made constant improvements. They used the Japanese word *kaizen*, which means "change for better," to name the principle they discovered.

Rather than just putting your nose to the grindstone and hustling, kaizen offers a way to do work that is done right and is fulfilling. It means you do the right things at the right moment, and you do them with the *hope of improvement* in mind.

So often we don't do things for improvement, we only do them for results. We want to make changes only when they will produce an immediate huge win. But if you shift your focus to smaller, incremental improvements, your successes will steadily increase.

For one thing, kaizen increases work flow, because people can see how their contributions affect the rest of the structure. Satisfaction increases as well as retention. Instead of running hard, they are running with passion, because they can see real results.

Kaizen also promotes healthy changes. Too often we only make changes in reaction to something not working. As you focus on incremental improvements, you can see smaller changes that need to be made before any issues arise. How much better will your team work together when they anticipate and avoid problems?

ChurchOS works on this principle. We believe in the power of incremental improvement. If you're hoping for overnight success or a quick fix, you won't find it. But if you commit to rigorous assessment and constant improvement, you will be amazed at how far and how quickly you can progress. You will also be surprised at how God meets you in your diligence and surprises you with unexpected victories.

How are you doing when it comes to constant improvement? Give yourself a grade from A to F. My grade: _____

ARE YOU READY?

How did you do overall? What was your overall grade? Remember, no one is expecting you to be perfect. Later on, we will familiarize you with the more fine-tuned evaluation process in ChurchOS. But for now, give yourself an overall grade.

Whether you scored yourself above average, failing, or somewhere in between, view this as a progress report, not the final exam! Don't get bogged down in the details just yet. Take it one step at a time and decide on this new approach to leadership, and it will help you understand ChurchOS. It might seem hard to clear out the old processes and systems (some of them you're not even consciously aware of), but clearing out the mechanism is necessary, even if time consuming. This isn't about trying something new just for the sake of trying it. This is about taking a step toward ongoing Great Commission activation and double kingdom impact. An Intentional Church needs Intentional Leaders.

NO MORE POPCORNING

THE CROSSING CHURCH — LAS VEGAS, NEVADA

Scott Whaley

At The Crossing, we had sharp leaders. We had great people with ministry experience, but we were *popcorning* great strategic movements without focus across our entire ministry platform. We also lacked accountability. We would start some things and they would go by the wayside. Because we were experiencing some growth, it wasn't as urgent to do things differently. We tended to have a buffet ministry mentality. The old logic used to be that if someone wanted to do something and lead it, let them do it. After we started ChurchOS, that changed. We are not running around and bumping into each other like we used to. When I had eight different strategies popping up, it required so much more work and resources. Now, we are about clarity and focus on our primary strategy. There has been a huge shift in our intentionality.

REMOVING BARRIERS

TRADERS POINT CHRISTIAN CHURCH—INDIANAPOLIS, INDIANA

Jim Stanley

One of our values is to lower barriers that keep people from Jesus. The biblical story that serves as our reference point is the paralytic man on the mat who is lowered to Jesus by his friends. The barrier they removed was a hole in the roof. They went to great lengths to remove the barrier to Jesus. Our whole operating principle on weekends is removing the barriers.

For more stories and case studies, please visit www.intentionalchurches.com.

TWO

EIGHT ChurchOS FUNDAMENTALS

But you will receive power when the Holy Spirit comes
upon you. And you will be my witnesses, telling people
about me everywhere—in Jerusalem, throughout
Judea, in Samaria, and to the ends of the earth.

—ACTS 1:8

Eastside Christian Church in Anaheim, California, has been on the
Outreach 100 fastest growing and largest church lists for several
years running. We had the privilege of working with the team at
Eastside to install the ChurchOS system. Even before we arrived, Gene
Appel, the senior pastor, and the executive team had already discovered
the power of adopting a simple-system approach to leadership. They
are clear about their evangelistic focus. They have routines for planning and visioning. They filter decisions through their vision-based
strategic lenses. They measure vision results through simple metrics.
And they have an incredible system for connecting the ONE, the lost
in their community, to the church, Jesus, and others.

How has Eastside seen such success? They have simplified ministry and returned to the basics. In the words of Pastor Appel, "We
determined that in order to reach more people we needed to do less.

Our effectiveness went up when we simplified." They represent some core beliefs of ChurchOS: simple is better, less is more, and we sometimes make church too hard.

ChurchOS is a comprehensive system that gets back to basics. It is practical, predictable, and sustainable with actions that are linked together to produce reliable, desirable, measurable, and, frankly, profound kingdom results.

> PRACTICAL: ChurchOS is practical by teaching every church leader how to utilize user-friendly tools to activate their church's unique vision. The tools unearth real strategies and create a plan to accomplish the Great Commission.
>
> PREDICTABLE: It is predictable because it is based on a rhythm that can be repeated year after year.
>
> SUSTAINABLE: It is sustainable because each church leader has a transferable common language, tools, and processes that creates a healthy culture. They repeatedly make more and better disciples.
>
> MEASURABLE: Finally, ChurchOS produces measurable results by activating the Great Commission Engine, refreshing vision, and plans for double impact again and again.

In this chapter we will lay out the fundamentals of the system with descriptions for each of them. These fundamentals represent the core code of ChurchOS. It runs on these kernels of substance. This book is built to take you through each component in practical depth.

Also, we have a feeling you often will refer back to this chapter, so don't skim it! This is the beginning of your journey into the common language of ChurchOS and becoming an Intentional Church.

Here is the core code and the eight fundamentals we will walk you through in this book.

- Fundamental #1: Six Domains of Church
- Fundamental #2: ChurchOS Living Toolbox

- Fundamental #3: Intentional Growth Planning (IGP)
- Fundamental #4: The Spiritual Battlefield
- Fundamental #5: ChurchOS Evaluation Standard
- Fundamental #6: ChurchOS Rating Method
- Fundamental #7: Four Helpful Lists
- Fundamental #8: ChurchOS Activation Assessment (Basic)

FUNDAMENTAL #1: SIX DOMAINS OF CHURCH

AN OVERVIEW OF EVERY CHURCH

One of the objectives of ChurchOS is to simplify church leadership in a helpful way. We created the Six Domains of Church to simplify a big-picture view of church leadership. It is important we start at the highest level of understanding about the local church. Each area matters, but it can be overwhelming to think about them all at once. These domains represent the sum total of church leadership—no matter the size, type, model, or approach in ministry. We've had many church leaders tell us this makes the local church easier to understand. Maybe you, too, will feel encouraged at the simplicity!

Let's break down each area with a simple description and a few clarifying questions. These questions are rhetorical for now, but we believe you will have a clear answer for them by the end of this book. Imagine if you did! Each area represents a domain of church leadership that must be addressed as you lead your church.

Great Commission Engine

In Matthew 28:19–20, every church is commanded by Christ to make more and better disciples. We use a tool that is a direct product of Jesus' command. We use it to walk you through a thorough assessment of the top seven Great Commission strategies every church must employ. We use Acts 2 and Luke 15, along with Matthew 28, to instruct us. The engine powers Great Commission activation. Some of the key questions for this domain are:

- How will we intentionally connect the lost to your church, Christ, and one another?
- Once we have reached the lost, how will we disciple them into devoted and growing followers of Jesus?
- How will we put people on mission with Christ and our church?

Activation

You could have a great plan for all of the other domains and still not activate the Great Commission. Activation requires measuring vision outcomes, establishing good routines and meetings, and assuring your decision-making model does not hold you back. Some of the key questions for this domain are:

- Do we have an agreed-upon set of vision metrics?
- How often are we meeting, and what do those meetings include?
- Who is responsible for what?
- How do we make decisions today while preparing for a new tomorrow?
- When do we get to celebrate?

Vision

Vision is necessary in church leadership. A God-born sense of tomorrow is both compelling and guiding for everyone on the team. It also creates healthy tension-producing insight and courageous decisions that lead to increased kingdom impact. Some of the key questions for this domain are:

- Who are we positioned to reach for Christ?
- Where is God leading us in the next three to five years?
- What would it look like to double our kingdom impact?
- How will we know we are making more and better disciples?
- Is this vision clear, compelling, and shared by all?
- How will we measure our vision?

Operations

Churches can't run without systems, processes, and routines. They are like the skeleton in a body, namely, you don't think about it much until it breaks down and hurts you. They must be proactively maintained. These include church data collection, facilities, hiring, finances, communications, and more. Just imagine if you didn't have a plan for these areas. Some key questions for this domain include:

- Are our systems the right size for today and tomorrow?
- What is holding us back or creating chaos?
- What new system do we need to implement?

- Have we documented our routines to create efficiency and scalability for growth?

Leaders

The church is made of people, not buildings. The mission is accomplished with and through people. Changed lives are both the product of our efforts and integral to the process of accomplishing the mission. This is a daunting challenge, and the key questions for this domain are quite obvious.

- Do we have the right people, and are they in the right roles for both today and tomorrow?
- What kind of team culture will govern our actions?
- What is our plan for developing leaders both for today's needs and tomorrow's challenges?

Action

Consistent, strategic action is difficult in the church. The rhythms of church are such that the near term dominates our planning, foresight, and daily lives. Sunday is always coming! Some of the key questions for this domain are:

- What must we act on today?
- What can our teams be doing right now?
- What do we need to be doing together? Alone?
- What will release the impact of our church in the next season?
- What do we need to be scouting for that's coming next?

FUNDAMENTAL #2: ChurchOS LIVING TOOLBOX

REPEATABLE STRATEGIC CONVERSATIONS

Now, let's look at the resources needed to run ChurchOS. We are constantly developing and adapting a set of tools that are integral to it. It is a wide range of powerful constructs that we call the Living Toolbox. The church is both an organization and an organism. It needs a set of tools that can grow and adapt as it grows.

What is a tool? A tool sets up a strategic conversation. It usually involves a visual representation and clarifying questions. It is typically facilitated by a neutral leader to garner a team's insight and elevated learning. Let's be honest, we've all left meetings wondering if anything was accomplished in them. Great tools create team-based dialogue that leads to incredible alignment and innovation. These guided constructs will create powerful and even paradigm-shifting conversations and plans.

ChurchOS Living Toolbox™

We have packaged just five of these tools in one-day workshops and seen amazing results. One participating church grew by more than 300 percent in one year, and another baptized more the following year than they had in the previous twenty years combined! They took courageous action because of the conversation and insights and then watched God move.

The Living Toolbox has grown to over forty-five tools that cover all Six Domains of Church, including people, vision, action, roadblocks, and more. ChurchOS is intended to be a total platform upon which your church can run, but the key is to learn the basics first. We are going to cover the basic system in this book. One day you will be using ChurchOS throughout your ministry in departments, campuses, board meetings, and church plants. We are also developing advanced and topical tools designed to be plug-and-play with the system similar to the way software works naturally with your computer's or phone's operating system.

FUNDAMENTAL #3: INTENTIONAL GROWTH PLANNING (IGP)

THE CORE PROCESS(OR) OF ChurchOS

Every operating system needs a core processor and code to run. At the heart of ChurchOS is a four-phase process called Intentional Growth Planning (IGP). It is the cycle through which God will lead you and your church. It uses tools from the Living Toolbox and revolves around the Great Commission Engine, the Six Domains of Church, and the big idea of double impact.

This book is built on the four phases of the IGP process. You are about to embark on a lap through the four phases: *discover, design, organize,* and *activate.* Hundreds of churches have used this simple cycle and the tools within each phase to build a plan that is changing their church and righteously growing their kingdom impact.

Here is the focus of each phase:

- DISCOVER today's Great Commission activation status
- DESIGN tomorrow's double kingdom vision, evangelistic focus, and engagement path
- ORGANIZE the next season's work to release your gospel potential and activate the Great Commission
- ACTIVATE the rhythm and routines that lead to continued Great Commission activation—more and better disciples

You may not notice it at first, but we are believers in beginning with lots of discovery before we design, organize, and activate a plan. We view discovery as the ascending of a team above the ministry in such a way that the past, present, and future all naturally come into sight. And they do! But note: this is through team *self*-discovery, not our discoveries revealed to the team. We spend a great amount of time in self-discovery each time we work with a church, and thus you will spend a good amount of time in this book doing the same.

The process is easy to learn and use. The more you engage it over time, the more natural it will become.

FUNDAMENTAL #4: THE SPIRITUAL BATTLEFIELD

A POWERFUL WORD PICTURE

The best visions use word pictures and analogies. Jesus taught in parables for a reason, namely, to connect his listeners' daily lives to the kingdom of God. He knew what we've discovered: analogies provide powerful insights. Once you start using ChurchOS, you'll find our tools often use pictures and visuals for added learning and impact. There's a reason for that. We will reference several throughout this book, but one analogy applies to the big picture of ChurchOS better than most.

The Spiritual Battlefield

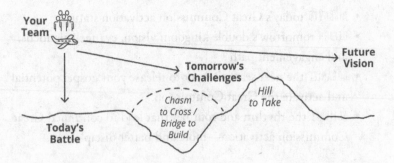

Take a close look at the figure above. It depicts several aspects of our reality as church leaders. It also represents the complex job of church leadership and how ChurchOS is built to help.

THE BATTLEFIELD. Scripture is clear that we are engaged in a spiritual battle. Specifically, in Ephesians 6, Paul said we do not fight "against flesh-and-blood enemies" (v. 12). That's so true, but it's easy to overlook. People will disappoint us, abandon us, and hurt us. But we are not fighting against *them*. There are forces at work behind the scenes—the rulers, authorities, and powers of a dark world—along with all forms of evil in the spiritual realm. We need to understand first the nature of the battle itself.

Deep insights occur when we grasp the nature of the battle. In 2 Kings 6, Elisha's enemy sent an army of horses and chariots to capture him. The prophet's servant was terrified and asked what they should do. Elisha then prayed for his servant's eyes to be opened to the real battle taking place (v. 17), and he saw God's forces outnumbering those of the enemy. God answered the prophet's prayer, and the servant's eyes were opened. This is just one evidence of the spiritual battle that rages around us and how God is with us on the battlefield at all times.

BATTLEFIELD SURVEY. We mentioned this earlier in this chapter. Diligent self-discovery is imperative in proactive church leadership. The battle is very real, and the physical realm often mirrors the spiritual. It takes insight to understand when this is the case. By honoring the discover phase of our core process, your team will ascend above the battle like a drone gathering perspective on a battlefield to discern what's objectively true. It takes discipline and effort to launch the drone and ascend to the altitude needed to conduct a thorough survey *while* you are fighting the battle! If you do this, many aspects of your church will come into clear view.

TODAY'S REALITY. In the thick of the battle, reality can be hard to discern. Issues can be obscured and opinions vary. The truth becomes clear as you ascend through great tools and conversation. Threads of continuity emerge as issues surface. You can even prioritize the issues and choose what must be fixed today and, sometimes more importantly, what can wait until tomorrow.

TOMORROW'S CHALLENGES. As your church advances through the power of the gospel, new challenges will emerge. The best time to prepare for those challenges is while you are engaged in today's battles. It takes courage to live in today's reality and work on tomorrow's challenges at the same time. Ephesians 6:10 encourages us to be strong. That's because God knows there are moments of weakness, times of trying, and opportunities for failure. By ascending above the battlefield, your conviction will grow and the plan will emerge.

FUTURE VISION. Vision can be difficult to discern, but it is critical for your team. Vision motivates, inspires, and directs. We will be discussing vision development later in this book and why we believe double vision is a frame for vision casting and planning. But don't miss it. In our experience, clear vision is developed through insights only seen by periodically ascending above the battlefield and looking to the horizon. You can develop a strong vision intuition and feel for the future. It's imperative in the changing landscape of our leadership that we develop great skills at routine visioning.

FUNDAMENTAL #5: ChurchOS EVALUATION STANDARD

OBJECTIFYING TODAY'S STATUS

Church leadership teams are poor evaluators. Your team may be skilled at it, but in our experience, most teams do not have an agreed-upon standard for evaluation. Intentional Churches do, however.

We have a standard for evaluation that is integral to ChurchOS. Healthy evaluation takes today's status into account without hedging. We must be honest and objectify today's status of our church in light of the Lord's command in Matthew 28 toward effective Great Commission activation and the future call of double impact. When we make these big ideas the gold standard for evaluation, God leads us to profound conclusions, convictions, and decisions.

Here's how you learn to evaluate with these big ideas in mind. Let's use a simple example, such as your small group ministry.

- What is today's status of our small group ministry?
- Is our small group ministry helping us to activate the Great Commission by making more and better disciples?
- Is our small group ministry ready to contribute to double kingdom impact?

We are going to give you a lot more context to make objective evaluation easier to understand. We find, over and over, church leaders evaluate wrongly or weakly, and we believe it's a top reason our churches get stuck or lose momentum.

FIVE POOR BUT COMMON EVALUATION STANDARDS

POOR STANDARD 1: PERSONAL PREFERENCE. As leaders, we cannot evaluate by our own personal opinions and preferences. Church can be a very personal subject, so this can be difficult. We must remove our prejudices from the criteria and do what's in the best interest of advancing the Lord's bride. This may be the most difficult evaluation trap to *not* fall into. The tendency to judge by our own standards is deeply engrained in us.

POOR STANDARD 2: PAST SUCCESS. We cannot evaluate only on the basis of past successes and expect to be relevant in the future. It's easy to rest on past victories and become complacent. Every church has had a high point and a low point, but we fight a battle in a world that is ever-changing and culturally evolving. Nostalgia can be fun. It's enjoyable to turn on an old movie, pull out a scrapbook or photo album, or catch the highlights of long-ago sports champions. But nostalgia is only about the past. Tomorrow's strategies may not look like those of yesterday or even today.

POOR STANDARD 3: GETTING BETTER. It's so easy to judge today's status by considering the progress already made. It's so important to stop from time to time and celebrate some accomplishments with your team, but that should never be an end goal. Leverage those times of celebration to find new ways of improvement while your heart is full and your motivation is high. How can you get better while measuring the success you've already obtained? Let those times be a motivation to keep going!

POOR STANDARD 4: COMPARISON. We all enjoy attending conferences, and it's both helpful and biblical to connect with other churches in your community. But be careful to focus on learning and encouragement during these opportunities instead of using them to compare your church to others. If your staff attends a conference and a speaker says the standard staff size and budget for his ministry is double yours, does that mean your approach is wrong? If a nearby church starts a recovery ministry, holds a summer VBS, or launches a food pantry, should you hurry to do the same? Every church is unique, and when you focus on comparison, you risk diluting your resources and diverting your energies from what is important to you and your ministry. Comparison is a poor and potentially dangerous way to measure success.

POOR STANDARD 5: ANECDOTAL EVIDENCE. A church of any size cannot rely on a story or two to frame its reality. It's not uncommon to walk the halls in most churches and hear thoughts, opinions, and feelings from others walking nearby. Their stories may represent something worth uncovering, but more likely they are not evidence of much. It's also easy to prove any point through anecdotal evidence. This is called *confirmation bias*, relying on data or stories that back up our argument and disprove the other side. As a pastor, you can come up with a story to defend any position. But just because you heard one story doesn't make it true for the rest of the church or necessarily provide reliable information for true discovery.

Maybe you can relate to First Baptist Church, Orlando, a legacy Southern Baptist church with a 150-year history. They've gone through an amazing transition from a white-collar, English-speaking church to a diverse church both socioeconomically and ethnically. In fact, 35 percent of their congregation's primary language is something other than English. Matthew Robinson, the pastor of administration at FBC Orlando, admitted their method of evaluation needed a facelift. "Before using these tools, there was a lack of ministry evaluation except for the anecdotal story. Our evaluation system used to be completely driven by story—the one story on how the weekend went or the one guy who had an amazing transformation. We liked feeling good and could justify almost anything because of the story. Having a vision for double impact changes things. Now we have a baseline of how to evaluate."

We are shamelessly going to try to change your evaluation standards. Developing a common framework for evaluating your ministry could be one of the single most important things you get from this book. It will create unprecedented alignment and unity for your team.

FUNDAMENTAL #6: ChurchOS RATING METHOD

SCORING TODAY'S STATUS

We believe a rating system, coupled with a unified evaluation standard, is a very important part of ChurchOS. In fact, we are big fans of developing a flash-grading system you can use prior to a deep-dive diagnosis. You will find rating a topic (like the previous small group ministry example) prior to detailed discussions will create a healthy tension that will drive great diagnostic discussions.

Here is the color-coded, simple rating system used throughout this book. It is one of several scoring systems we use in ChurchOS and very simple to use. Please take the evaluation standards we just discussed into account. You must combine the evaluation standards with the rating system to produce great team insights.

We use a color-based scoring system as follows:

RED: A red rating means the item is not in position to activate the Great Commission or drive double kingdom impact. It is potentially broken or barely functioning to these standards. It demands attention.

YELLOW: A yellow rating means the item affects Great Commission activation and double kingdom impact but has room for improvement. It is not at its top level of effectiveness. It needs further action to become optimal.

GREEN: A green rating means the item activates the Great Commission and drives double kingdom impact. It is effective and healthy. It might have room for improvement, but that space is far less than a yellow item. Ensure this item has the resources and attention it needs.

We will implement this scoring system later in the book and give more details and practical examples of how it works.

FUNDAMENTAL #7: FOUR HELPFUL LISTS

A SWISS-ARMY-KNIFE DIAGNOSTIC TOOL

It's one thing to have a common evaluation standard and rating system, but you need a device to capture details, drive insights, and make decisions. We use a diagnostic tool called Four Helpful Lists (with permission from the Paterson Center in Fort Collins, Colorado). It is simple but powerful and has become somewhat common among leaders and teams.

Four Helpful Lists	
Right (Amplify)	Wrong (Fix)
Missing (Add)	Confused (Clarify)

© Paterson Center LLC, Used by permission.

The tool is based on four simple, internal-facing questions and can be drawn on an easel pad or a whiteboard in front of your team or during a meeting. You can draw it as a four-box design like the figure here, or you can create four columns on a whiteboard or two easel pad sheets taped on a wall. You simply discuss the answers to the four questions and take summary bullet-style notes as you go through the corresponding boxes or columns.

Here are the questions that drive the captured details:

- *What is right?* (What is working that we can amplify or leverage?)
- *What is wrong?* (What must be fixed?)
- *What is missing?* (What do we need to add to increase our impact?)
- *What is confused?* (What do we need to clarify?)

We will use the Four Helpful Lists as our evaluation tool as we go through this book. We will give you more instructions and examples of how it can be used. The context makes all the difference to the outcomes and insights.

We recommend you make Four Helpful Lists your team-wide diagnostic standard. For many churches, this tool has brought about congruency in evaluation as well as empowered all the members of a team to have a voice in evaluation.

Hal Mayer, the executive pastor at Church at the Springs in Ocala, Florida, reported:

All of our staff uses Four Helpful Lists to evaluate things. We will do a special weekend and then walk through these questions. Our children's ministry might try something new and use it as well. It is one of the most helpful tools to bring engagement and discussion. Our student ministry leaders even use this with volunteers. It allows you to get more perspective. You don't ask the cook how the food tastes. They think it's wonderful! If you are only asking staff, it may or may not be right. We use these questions to gain more perspective.

Here's a great tip from Pastor Mayer: start with what is right.

Truth is, we need to focus on what we are doing right. If you just focus on what is wrong, you will stop doing some of the things that were really right and miss it. Sometimes we talk about all of it at once. The beauty is putting the notes up and then stepping to the side and truly evaluating.

FUNDAMENTAL #8: ChurchOS ACTIVATION ASSESSMENT (BASIC)

HOW ARE YOU DOING TODAY AS AN INTENTIONAL CHURCH?

We are going to give you the *basic* ChurchOS Activation Assessment. Don't worry, we will give you the *complete* assessment at the end of the book, once you've fully worked with and integrated these concepts, after you've been through all four phases of Intentional Growth Planning in this book. Some benchmarks might be difficult to understand, but you can likely infer the teaching and principles that undergird them. We are convinced about these benchmarks, because we've seen simple improvements in just one area lead to tremendous momentum. These twenty-one benchmarks are at the heart of ChurchOS. They will deliver sustained Great Commission activation through diligent implementation and evaluation.

Before you begin, remember our evaluation standards and scoring. We are immediately putting them into practice by judging our scoring against the big ideas of sustained Great Commission activation and double kingdom impact.

Hint: If you use this assessment methodology with those big ideas in mind, you should never get a perfect score, because double vision is an ever-evolving big idea. As the horizon shifts, the scores should change, because your dreams are getting bigger and your goals loftier. More on that later in the book!

Let's go. Grade yourself as a team. Track your scores in your journal or on a separate piece of paper.

Place an X in the box that represents your grade. (R = red, Y = yellow, G = green; refer to our rating method.)

	Question	R (1 point)	Y (3 points)	G (6 points)
1	MISSION: We understand the mission of the local church is the Great Commission and have restated it clearly in our own terms.			
2	VISION: We have a clear five-year vision and we refresh it every twelve to twenty-four months.			
3	EVALUATION: Our team has common, objective evaluation standards and methods.			
4	THE LAST 10 PERCENT: We are deeply honest about our church and are objective about its plans and strategies.			
5	THE GREAT COMMISSION ENGINE: We understand the top five strategies every church must address.			
6	PRIORITIES FOR IMPACT: Our ministry strategies are prioritized and reviewed annually (at least). We have no sacred cows.			
7	FOCUS ON OUR ONE: Our church is built to reach and develop the lost.			
8	ENGAGEMENT PATHWAY: We have a defined pathway that is built to connect the lost to our church.			
9	ACTIVATION DASHBOARD: We have a clearly defined vision activation heads-up display that is owned and reviewed regularly.			

10	THE NEXT SEASON'S WORK: We are clear about the work that must be accomplished in the next season to release the gospel potential of our church.			
11	STRUCTURE AND ROLES: Our roles and organization chart make sense, and we know how to measure individual success. We know how to manage strategic work on the way to double kingdom impact.			
12	MEETINGS: We know how to run great meetings. Our meeting agendas make sense and are efficient.			
13	COMMON LANGUAGE: We use consistent language and definitions that are owned by pastors, staff, leaders, and volunteers.			
14	IGP DEPLOYMENT AND TRAINING: We have Intentional Growth Plans established across our ministries.			
15	ACTIVATION OWNERSHIP: We have identified a champion (activator) who holds us accountable to Great Commission activation.			
16	SILVER BULLETS: We know how to plug in the latest ministry solutions and not chase silver bullets.			
17	GOVERNANCE AND DECISION-MAKING: The model for our leadership structure makes sense, and we know how to make decisions effectively and with appropriate speed.			
18	GENEROSITY: We are effective at regularly casting vision, inspiring generosity, and calling for increasing financial sacrifice.			
19	LEADERSHIP DEVELOPMENT: We know how to develop leaders at all levels and can clearly identify who is on mission with us.			

20	PRAYER: We have a proactive plan for prayer to release the power of the Holy Spirit. We know prayer and the Holy Spirit fuel Great Commission activation and evangelistic growth.			
21	MULTIPLYING: We are convicted and praying about and planning for how God can use us to help other churches activate the Great Commission.			

Our score in each area is:

Total number of red marks x 1 = _____

Total number of yellow marks x 3 = _____

Total number of green marks x 6 = _____

Our grand total is _____

Here is the key to the assessment. Chart your score.

0	60	120
Red (<22)	Yellow (22–60)	Green (61–120)
(Mark an X below where you scored in the continuum.)		

The scoring is weighted because there is incredible power in the principles beneath these twenty-one benchmarks. If you improve only slightly in one of these areas, it can have a great impact in your church. We've seen it!

From this one assessment you can begin your discovery process. **Warning!** This is just the beginning. We need many more conversations to truly see the threads of continuity and themes emerge. Discovery takes patience. Do not fall victim to drawing conclusions too quickly, trying to fix it all, or making short-sighted decisions.

Let's learn something from this next exercise.

In a journal or separate piece of paper:

- List the benchmarks marked with a red X.
- List the benchmarks marked with a yellow X.
- List the benchmarks marked with a green X.

As a team, talk through the items and circle the one the team feels rises to the surface in the red and yellow lists as the biggest roadblocks to kingdom progress and Great Commission activation. Sometimes these conversations can be difficult, and we will give you more help as we go along on how to have these discussions. But give it a try!

Do the same for the items listed in the green list. In this list, however, you can have two discussions: What is the strongest item in the list (something we can leverage)? What is lower in rank and could use improvement? Circle those items.

Remember, we aren't making any decisions yet! We are just beginning the journey of self-discovery as a team. This kind of team-based Great Commission planning represents a new day in church leadership. Let's begin the journey through Intentional Growth Planning and on to becoming an Intentional Church.

ADVICE FROM THE TRENCHES

THE OAKS CHURCH—RED OAK, TEXAS

Mark Brewer

Scott, our senior pastor, is a vision caster, and my role as executive pastor is to be the vision driver. Depending on the organization and size, sometimes you have to do the leading and the driving. While Scott's role is the why and the what, my role is discovering the how and when.

When I pulled the trigger on implementing ChurchOS, it was really more for me as executive pastor than anything else. I recognized I had it in my wheelhouse to develop an operating system and culture here, but it would be five or six years before I would feel solid about it. If we wanted to get there quicker, I needed some help. Bringing in an outside voice and system was originally about pursuing things quicker. I needed something bigger, badder, and more helpful that everyone in the organization could say yes to.

We are a little over four years into our first lap. It has been a rocky journey, not because of ChurchOS, but because of us. Honestly, the first couple of years we learned about the system but thought we were smarter than what was presented. We tried to "Oaks-ify" what we learned, and I think a lot of churches can do that, especially if they are innovative. We absorb ideas too quickly and immediately try to redeploy. That is one of the reasons the first couple of years were so clunky for us. But we stuck with it, and we are starting to really see that this is the operating system by which we will function. Our culture is decidedly different because of ChurchOS, to the point we are intentionally handing this off to the next generation.

JUST DOING MORE JUST DOESN'T WORK

FIRST CHRISTIAN CHURCH—MORRIS, ILLINOIS

Scott Zorn and Todd Thomson

Prior to our journey of ChurchOS and focusing on the Great Commission Engine, we operated on the philosophy that somehow we could squeeze out better results by doing the same things, just more of them. That was a well-established pattern and strategy. We probably had over a hundred different things people could do, and they were not prioritized. Now, we have trimmed down and have a clear message. For instance, we don't do men's ministry. It wasn't high-functioning or contributing to double impact, so we cut it out. The hard truth is that big decisions or shifts come with loss, but it's worth it.

For more stories and case studies, please visit www.intentionalchurches.com.

PHASE ONE:
DISCOVER

The Intentional Growth Planning core process of ChurchOS includes four phases: discover, design, organize, and activate. As a discipline, take some time for thorough discovery. This takes patience. Your team must objectively assess your ministry to discover the truth about today so we can make a great plan for tomorrow. To drive honest conversation and team-based self-discovery, we are going to use some helpful analogies.

THREE

THE GREAT COMMISSION ENGINE (PART I)

Upon this rock I will build my church, and all
the powers of hell will not conquer it.

—MATTHEW 16:18

We are big believers in the power of self-discovery. Like good
counseling, it can be truly transformative; however, team-based
self-discovery is especially challenging. We have learned over the years
that it takes a frame or paradigm to begin with. If you don't frame your
discovery, then any opinion seems relevant and potentially coequal
with the next. How many meetings have been derailed because we
can't agree on the simplest definitions and purposes behind what we
do in church?

We use a simplifying analogy called the Great Commission
Engine as the anchoring frame at the highest level of ChurchOS and
Intentional Growth Planning. This profound simplicity has helped
many teams begin the journey of honest self-assessment in light of
the Great Commission. It rests on some of the most famous passages
in the Bible.

THREE IMPORTANT SCRIPTURES

We combine insights from three passages to form the Great Commission Engine. They represent our return to biblical basics.

MATTHEW 28:16–20

Our foundational passage for the Great Commission Engine is Matthew 28:16–20. Just because you've heard a scripture over and over again doesn't mean you have clarity on it. Sometimes it takes a deeper look. So even if you have it memorized, you should read the entirety of Matthew 28:16–20 again *and* slowly, noting the thoughts and actions of the disciples and soaking in this directive from Jesus.

> Then the eleven disciples went to Galilee, to the mountain where Jesus had told them to go. When they saw him, they worshiped him; but some doubted. Then Jesus came to them and said, "All authority in heaven and on earth has been given to me. Therefore go and make disciples of all nations, baptizing them in the name of the Father and of the Son and of the Holy Spirit, and teaching them to obey everything I have commanded you. And surely I am with you always, to the very end of the age." (NIV)

There is both a powerful directive and a great encouragement in this passage. First, the disciples wanted to follow Jesus, but some still doubted. Jesus knew this and still invited them on his mission and they followed. Have you ever had doubts but still taken steps to follow him? We have! And then Jesus spoke with convicting clarity to his leaders about the church's mission for all times. Each and every church (and leader) is called to *go* and *grow* its kingdom impact in Jesus' name.

We call this Great Commission activation, and it is this original mission statement that has guided gospel-centered churches for more than two thousand years. It's also a brilliant strategy that leads to ever-increasing impact. The church is to:

- Go to the world
- Preach the gospel
- Baptize the uninitiated
- Teach them to obey
- Repeat the cycle!

What a simple, repeatable, and clear mission Christ gave us. Hopefully, you have restated this mission in your own words and memorized it as a team. Did you notice that little promise at the end of this passage? He promised to be with us always as we execute his mission—even though at times we will be filled with doubt and limited by our human perspective. We have no fear because he is on mission with us!

ACTS 2:42–47

In Acts 2 we read about the Holy Spirit's coming to empower the believers and Peter's great first sermon that launched the church. Then we catch a glimpse of the local church in operation in verses 42–47. This picture becomes a model for how the first church put the Great Commission of Jesus into action.

> They devoted themselves to the apostles' teaching and to fellowship, to the breaking of bread and to prayer. Everyone was filled with awe at the many wonders and signs performed by the apostles. All the believers were together and had everything in common. They sold property and possessions to give to anyone who had need. Every day they continued to meet together in the temple courts. They broke bread in their homes and ate together with glad and sincere hearts, praising God and enjoying the favor of all the people. And the Lord added to their number daily those who were being saved. (NIV)

What a beautiful picture of the church! Here is what we see:

- Commitment to gather and learn from the apostles
- Divesting and giving generously to each other where there is need

- Gathering in homes and developing deep relationships
- Enjoying favor, gladness, and the fruits of deep sincerity
- Awe abounding as God moved through the apostles
- Natural growth of a contagious, loving movement

We believe this early church was more than a great story. We believe it represents a model that has endured for two thousand years. This model is at the heart of the Great Commission Engine and ChurchOS. We also believe these words should describe our modern-day churches, albeit with twenty-first-century skin on them.

In this chapter we are going to walk you through our thinking and teaching on this model. In the next chapter, we are going to put some skin on the teaching and apply it to today's church so we can begin our evaluation.

LUKE 15

In Luke 15 Jesus described what a biblical search-and-rescue mission looks like. Jesus told three stories that give radical emphasis on seeking what is lost: a lost coin, a lost sheep, and a lost son. Look at the lost sheep, since Jesus talked a lot about being a shepherd.

> Suppose one of you has a hundred sheep and loses one of them. Doesn't he leave the ninety-nine in the open country and go after the lost sheep until he finds it? And when he finds it, he joyfully puts it on his shoulders and goes home. Then he calls his friends and neighbors together and says, "Rejoice with me; I have found my lost sheep." I tell you that in the same way there will be more rejoicing in heaven over one sinner who repents than over ninety-nine righteous persons who do not need to repent. (vv. 4–7 NIV)

We told you ChurchOS is centered on the ONE. We have coined this language from this story in Luke 15. You will hear us refer to the ONE and the Ninety-Nine. The ONE represents the one who is lost.

The Ninety-Nine represents the church family or flock. We are called to be on mission with the Shepherd.

WHY SO MUCH EMPHASIS ON THE ONE?

First, emphasis on the ONE is Jesus' way. Over and over we are reminded he came to seek and to save the lost. It was his primary mission. Second, we believe a focus on evangelism and reaching the lost will grow deeply committed disciples. (Read that sentence again!) One of God's greatest growth strategies is to ask you to focus on reaching the lost. It will grow you, and it will grow the church. Incredible maturity is required when you realize the church is not here just to serve you and your needs.

We've all heard the telltale signs of a church turned inward, unintentionally developing Christian consumers.

- "I'm not being fed."
- "I don't feel like this is *my* church anymore."
- "This is fine if you are new to Jesus, but I need something deeper."
- Fill in the blank.

Jesus embodied what we are about to cover. He is the author and creator of this framework. He went preaching and teaching, living in rich community, and living a fully surrendered life. He engaged people directly, inviting them into relationship with him and the Father. This is not only what Jesus said to do and what the early church did in response, but it is how he lived. Why would we, as leaders, live any other way? Why would we lead any other way?

The church's mission is not to make us comfortable. There is power in the discomfort. Seth Godin noted, "Discomfort brings engagement and change. Discomfort means you're doing something that others were unlikely to do, because they're hiding out in the comfortable zone."[1]

The church exists to be on Christ's mission of seeking and saving the lost—the ONE—as uncomfortable as that might be. We will bring you back to this idea and what it means for our churches. We are also going to walk you through how to have this defining conversation as a team.

INTRODUCTION: THE GREAT COMMISSION ENGINE (GCE)

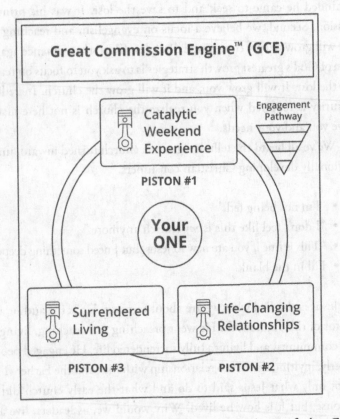

Let's step through a three-piston-engine analogy of the Great Commission Engine. We are asking you to embrace it for now and let us describe it to you. You might be surprised how meaningful, simple, and powerful it is.

First, yes, it's a three-piston engine, and there really is such a thing. In fact, three-piston engines are making a big comeback! The Geo Metro was one of the first cars to be powered by one, and we all know how that went. Today, the powerful BMW i8 is one of many on the road today. We've also heard the three-piston setup is in Jet Skis, generators, and construction equipment. Here's the reality of these engines: they are uniquely synergistic systems. When one piston doesn't fire well, substantial horsepower is lost. You would think that if one piston didn't fire, you would lose only 33 percent horsepower. The reality, however, is you lose much more than that. The synergy of the system is greatly hindered because of the nature of its design. Each piston is significantly responsible for the engine's effectiveness and relies on the next piston to hand off the energy to the next. These handoffs maintain the rotational momentum of the engine and the consistent delivery of power.

We think it's the same for the Great Commission Engine. Could it be that if one of the components isn't firing well, we lose tremendous gospel impact? If one piston isn't healthy and handing off its energy to the next, is Great Commission activation in jeopardy? We can tell you from experience this is likely true. Keep this in mind as you learn about the components, thinking of the scriptural purpose of each.

Let's put the components together, along with the powerful purpose of each.

CRANKSHAFT: THE ONE

Let's start by describing how a three-piston engine works. In the middle is the crankshaft. As this turns it powers all the other parts of the car, including turning the wheels and powering all the electronics. Pistons are aligned along the crankshaft. When the first one fires, it pushes down and turns the crankshaft. Then the second and third fire in rapid succession. As the second fires, it pulls the first piston back into place. When the third fires, it brings the second piston into alignment. And so on. This is how three-piston engines create synergy. The firing of each piston doesn't just rotate the crankshaft, it actually creates momentum and keeps the other two moving as well.

Every engine revolves around a heavy center point, namely, the crankshaft. That's what's important. So let's ask: What is the most important part of your church? What is its center point? The Great Commission Engine must be built around a central idea. We propose that central idea is reaching the lost, the ONE.

You need to understand two things about the ONE in Luke 15. First, the ONE is lost. It may seem the shepherd is leaving ninety-nine sheep in danger just to find one lost sheep, but the distinction is that the ninety-nine are *no longer* lost! Your ONE is anyone in your Relational Reach Zone who does not have a relationship with the Great Shepherd, Jesus Christ.

Second, the shepherd did not decide to search for the lost sheep based on any thought of profit and loss. He had ninety-nine sheep. What difference would one more make? An eternity of difference! At least to the ONE. The point is, no matter how many people have been impacted by your church and ministry so far, it only increases your opportunity for double impact!

The ONE is in the center of the Great Commission Engine because the ONE is the central part of its mission. Jesus' goal for us is not to find those who are already in relationship with him to add to our church but to seek out and find those who are lost. Growth is natural when the ONE is your focus.

> CRANKSHAFT: THE ONE. We are on mission with Christ. He said he came to seek and save the lost. Then he told us to go make disciples, baptize, and teach. Your Great Commission Engine revolves around the ONE.

PISTON #1: CATALYTIC WEEKEND EXPERIENCE

Let's circle back to Acts 2. The important passage for double impact is found at the end of the chapter: "And the Lord added to their number daily those who were being saved" (v. 47 NIV). Maybe you grew up in a church where someone being saved was a rare occurrence.

For double-impact churches, it happens routinely, maybe even weekly or daily. What does it take to get to that point?

The first step is to rely on the catalytic teaching and worship in a weekend church service. Notice the early church met regularly in the temple courts. These were areas around the temple proper. Many teachers gathered here with their disciples. The apostles decided to do the same. They understood that meeting regularly was vital to the health of their entire body (Heb. 10:25).

What did they do in the temple courts? "They devoted themselves to the apostles' teaching" (Acts 2:42 NIV). In other words, they gathered and listened as those who had closely followed Jesus told stories about him, repeated his teachings, and preached Spirit-led sermons. They used the foolishness of preaching to change their world.

Imagine the other groups nearby, the ones who had already heard about Jesus but only knew him as a teacher who had been executed by the Romans. Sure, there were rumors he had come back from the grave. But were they true? Surely these people didn't believe that!

It was that foolishness, that willingness to tell the truth that the early church experienced, that touched the lives of those who considered themselves to be the most educated. As they met, they also worshiped. This led to "wonders and signs" (v. 43 NIV) that confirmed their words and attracted even more to know Jesus. What Jesus had predicted was coming true: "When I am lifted up . . . [I] will draw all people to myself" (John 12:32 NIV).

This is the first piston firing, the spark that ignites! It is catalytic because it starts the engine and creates momentum.

PISTON #1: CATALYTIC WEEKEND EXPERIENCE. **Preaching saves people. If Christ is lifted up, he will draw people to him. With the Holy Spirit involved, this is a powerful, catalytic, and spiritually explosive experience.**

PISTON #2: LIFE-CHANGING RELATIONSHIPS

Outside of those services in the temple courts, all of those first Christians continued to gather. You could describe it in one word: *relationship*. But they found something powerful in these relationships, something greater than anything they had ever experienced before.

Acts 2 says, "They broke bread in their homes and ate together with glad and sincere hearts" (v. 46 NIV). That last phrase can also be translated "hearts that are truly open." There were no areas closed off. There were no followers who isolated themselves.

True discipleship can only happen in the context of relationship. Weekend services are important, especially to help new believers make commitments to follow Christ. But the Ninety-Nine will also be catalyzed to respond because of the power of the Holy Spirit. What happens afterward is the true process of disciple-making, and it can't happen all alone. It must be done by connecting to others.

Faith may come by hearing (Rom. 10:17), but that's just the beginning. True growth comes from relationship. The spark of the first piston sets growth in motion in the next. And this is where the synergy of the Great Commission Engine really comes into play. When we meet together, we are helping to pull those who are coming behind us as we are being pulled along by those ahead of us.

> PISTON #2: LIFE-CHANGING RELATIONSHIPS. The gospel and discipleship are relational topics. Disciples are best made in the context of relationships. The Holy Spirit works through relationships in a unique way. We are better together.

PISTON #3: SURRENDERED LIVING

The "truly open hearts" of Acts 2:46 were focused on one thing: generosity. And they practiced it radically! Luke used words like "together" and "in common" to describe the outpouring of their hearts. And the result? "They sold property and possessions to give to anyone who had need" (v. 45 NIV). It's difficult to imagine that level of generosity in today's culture.

Such charity can only come by continual commitment to increasing surrender, and surrendering to God is a lifelong process. It can't happen overnight. We must continue to find new ways to live it out.

How does God use surrender in our lives to change our lives? It gets back to the synergy we mentioned before. Our weekend services draw people into the body of Christ. Meeting house to house is how we continually grow. Now, as we live these things out, it sparks a new missional direction in our lives.

This is the essence of the gospel message. Not being served, but serving as Jesus did, by giving up our own lives for others (Mark 10:45). We can never expect to see life change until we are willing to give up our own lives. The generosity of the Ninety-Nine with their time, talent, treasure, and attention is pivotal to Great Commission activation.

This can't be done on our own, though. We need the power of the Holy Spirit to be active in our lives on a daily basis. He moves us into spaces of trusting in him. He convicts us when we mess up, but he also convinces us of what's right—to be generous when it can make an impact. He gives us courage to step out of our comfort zones and into our reach zones. When we are walking in the Spirit, life change and surrender are common.

PISTON #3: SURRENDERED LIVING. **God uses the application of the gospel to our lives to change us and make us more selfless over time. He uses this life-changing surrender to also build his church and accomplish his purposes.**

THE ENGAGEMENT PATHWAY

Before we move on, let's look at one of the primary systems of ChurchOS and the Great Commission Engine: the Engagement

Pathway. As we discover the synergy within the model, this system sticks out because of its importance.

We hold a conviction around connecting people to each other and to Christ. Making disciples was not done by broadcasting but by one-on-one commitments. The lesson Jesus taught us in Luke 15 is one of personal engagement, not large-scale seeking. The Acts 2 story includes the phrase "added to their number." Even that speaks of making it personal.

It's easy to get swept up in the numbers in that story; however, each number represents a single person. That single person was won to Christ through the actions of a single person or a small group of people. It is such a simple concept that we often overlook it now.

The culture in which we live often goes against this. What was once intuitive now needs to be intentional. The Engagement Pathway encourages us to first connect other people with us, not by having a winning personality but through simple, intuitive, and personal steps of connection. Next, we connect them to Jesus. Then we connect with one another for growth and discipleship, and then repeat the process.

Again, this process is incredibly simple, and yet we see churches miss it. Those we are reaching are accustomed to staying disconnected. They bounce around so easily. You must engage and connect them if you want to double your kingdom impact.

> ENGAGEMENT PATHWAY. **Engaging with and connecting to the ONE is paramount. If we do not connect them to us, Christ, and one another, we aren't on mission with Christ.**

THE CHASSIS: LEADERS AND OPERATIONS

Just like a high-powered engine, the Great Commission Engine needs a strong chassis to hold it. Without that, it's doing little more than taking up space on the garage floor. The church has seen plenty of problems throughout history when it comes to inadequate infrastructure. In fact, it happened pretty quickly.

One example is in Acts 6. As the number of Christians grew, the need to serve widows increased, but there was a problem in the system. The Jewish Christians seemed to ignore the Greek Christians. The lack of a strong infrastructure was creating cracks in the church.

To fix the issue, the apostles leaned into strong teams, convictions, and values. This created a chassis of sorts that addressed concerns while allowing the engine to continue moving forward. First, they found some gifted Greek Christians to solve the problem (v. 3). Next, they addressed their lack of correct convictions. They held high principles when it came to teaching (v. 2), but they overlooked the importance of equity. Finally, they shifted their values to include accepting all people, regardless of race or heritage. It was a monumental moment in the life of the early church.

Take an honest look at your current team, values, and operational systems. Are they right-sized and aligned? Is there anything lacking? Could you improve in one area? For the Great Commission Engine to deliver kingdom impact, you need these systems to be strong and intact.

FUEL: THE GOSPEL, THE HOLY SPIRIT, AND PRAYER

An engine will only run if it has fuel to feed it. What is the fuel of the GCE? We think of it in terms of three sources. First, the gospel message is the indispensable ingredient. Without the truth of the life, death, resurrection, and ascension of Jesus Christ, none of this really matters. We're not much more than a social club or another nonprofit. But when we put the gospel into action, it has power (Rom. 1:16).

Next, we can do nothing short of the Holy Spirit's presence in our lives. That goes for individuals but more so for the church. The Greek word for power is *dunamis,* and much is made of the correlation to the word *dynamite.* Although they didn't have explosives in those days, it's telling that the same word was used to explain that dynamic power at work. When you allow the Holy Spirit to have free reign in your ministry, you are unleashing explosive power!

Finally, we must prioritize prayer. That's because prayer is a verbal act of surrender to God. We surrender our plans to his wisdom. We surrender our ambition to his will. We surrender our pride to his glory. When prayer is a focus, the engine is fueled to the max.

This engine is under the hood of your church! The beautiful reality is that you as the leaders are the driver. You get to decide what to do and where to take your ministry, but the power to get you there is contained in the simple model from Acts 2. We know the components of the Great Commission Engine working together will power your church forward. They will advance and grow your church.

MAKE IT YOUR OWN

Many churches have already identified a three-pronged strategic description of some type that they use to describe mission or vision. Hopefully, the Great Commission Engine can help you see where and how they fit, the underlying purpose for each, and how they must work synergistically and systematically to power your gospel impact.

Gene Appel and the team at Eastside Christian Church in Anaheim, California, have some language and strategies that already align the Great Commission Engine. They titled the first piston "Pursue God," the second is dubbed "Build Community," and the third piston is named "Unleash Compassion." Eastside is a very strategic ministry with clear plans for each of these components. The insight the Great Commission Engine brings is the paramount reality that these core strategy buckets actually revolve around the ONE. Furthermore, of top concern in this fast-growing church is the strategy to connect their ONE with an incredibly efficient Engagement Pathway. They have made the GCE their own and use the model as a central tool to keep their entire team clear and focused.

Appel shared, "Our big vision is to reach 1 percent of the population within a twenty-mile radius of our church. It gives me great joy when I hear the average Eastsider say the words, 'Pursue, Build, Unleash' or repeat our 1 percent vision. When the average attender says that, you know you are staying on top of it."

Here are a few examples from churches that made the Great Commission Engine their own through unique labels to create a common language and ownership:

Piston 1	Piston 2	Piston 3
Connect	Grow	Serve
Charge Up	Plug In	Live Out
Worship	Group	Give

We are going to walk you through the practical side of these components and apply them in more depth to your ministry. Do not miss the point here: each of these components has a powerful purpose, and no matter the label, we as leaders must respond categorically with plans that apply to each one.

BACK TO BASICS AND BALANCE

We've discovered the Great Commission Engine is useful in discussing an interesting dynamic of the past few decades in church leadership. If you've been around a while (like we have), you've seen some waves come and go. These waves have taken the form of church leadership models with nicknames like *attractional*, *communal*, and *missional*. Part of my (Bart) life story was searching for the perfect model and then realizing the only true model comes from Scripture, specifically Acts 2. The Great Commission Engine explains this labeling phenomena, and surprisingly it's directly tied to the ever-evolving generational landscape.

These models and movements are the result of the overemphasis of the Acts 2 model depicted in the Great Commission Engine. Generally speaking, the overemphasis of Piston 1 was owned by the baby boomers and labeled the *attractional* church model. The overemphasis of Piston 2 came by way of Generation X and was labeled the *communal* or *house church* model. And the overemphasis of Piston 3 was led by millennials and labeled the *missional* or *incarnational* model.

We are convinced that any overemphasis creates an imbalance in the Great Commission Engine. When that happens, like we said earlier in the chapter, gospel horsepower is significantly reduced.

I (Doug) have firsthand experience in a church that made the mistake of overemphasizing one component of the engine. I was a leader in a church that attempted to launch and use the communal/house church model in Las Vegas. We had the best intentions and a growing network of house churches, but the ministry eventually imploded because we were out of balance. We didn't respect the discipleship power of Piston 1 (Catalytic Weekend Experience) and Piston 3 (Surrendered Living), and we certainly had a hard time keeping the ONE in focus. We plateaued, declined, and eventually closed our doors. We enjoyed the favor of God and others for a while, but eventually focusing on one piston was not enough to sustain our Great Commission activation.

We believe in each of the previous movements, but each generation was reacting to the one before it. Here's how it happened.

Boomer said, "Hey, we can learn a lot from business and marketing principles and apply them to our church leadership. The prospective customer is most likely going to walk through the door on a weekend, so let's place most of our resources there!"

Gen Xer said, "You silly boomers! Bigger isn't better. Closer is better. And customer? We need relationships and generational commiseration. Community is where it's at, and the gathering is just a by-product of rich relationships and shared life, anyway."

Millennial said, "You lazy Xers and crazy boomers. If we took just half the money we put into a building and got off our rumps, we could do so much good in the world. Only impact matters. Everything else—including established institutions—is to be questioned."

Sound familiar?

We are calling for Intentional Churches to return to balance, and we believe there is great hope in the coming generations of church leadership. All of the components in the Great Commission Engine are important, and we can learn from the reactions of the generations to one another and not repeat the mistake of overemphasizing any one piston. We may need to focus on one component or subcomponent of the GCE at a time, and we may never achieve perfection, but we can strive for balance and use it as a tool to objectify the status of our church's most important strategies. We'll show you how in the next chapter.

RIPPLE EFFECT

EASTSIDE CHRISTIAN CHURCH—ANAHEIM, CALIFORNIA

Gene Appel

We have a high Latino population, so the matriarch in the family drives a lot of what the family does. Knowing this, our ONE is a thirty-three-year-old female. We felt she was the key to unlocking the man in her life and the whole family. She would be the one who would nudge the others forward. We actually thought, "What's the kind of stuff a woman can use to interest the man in her life?"

She is influential, and through her, we see the extended family. We often hear how one woman was baptized, then her sister, then their dad or aunt. We aren't necessarily female-driven, but we plan services, series, and events that capture her attention to want to share with the man in her life. I often go into the MOPS ministry and make the pitch as to why they need to bring the man in their life to our services, especially at

Christmastime. I tell them, "I am here to help you reach your guy! If you can get him here, this is what I am going to say and do."

DON'T COME TO CHURCH THIS WEEK

CROSSTOWER CHURCH—SALT LAKE CITY, UTAH

Randy Clay

We began encouraging our ministry team leaders to visit a different church every six weeks—and the stranger the better! We tell them to go to a place that is completely foreign to them and see how they feel. A lot of them come back realizing how important it is to welcome guests, know where the bathrooms are, and how to get help. On the upside, if they visit a great church, they will bring back at least one really good idea. (We have stolen a lot of good ideas!) It also keeps us focused on the ONE as ministry team leaders.

For more stories and case studies, please visit
www.intentionalchurches.com.

FOUR

THE GREAT COMMISSION ENGINE (PART 2)

They devoted themselves to the apostles' teaching and to fellowship,
to the breaking of bread and to prayer. Everyone was filled with awe
at the many wonders and signs performed by the apostles. All the
believers were together and had everything in common. They sold
property and possessions to give to anyone who had need. Every
day they continued to meet together in the temple courts. They
broke bread in their homes and ate together with glad and sincere
hearts, praising God and enjoying the favor of all the people. And
the Lord added to their number daily those who were being saved.

—ACTS 2:42–47 NIV

S he was standing in line and weeping. What line? The line waiting
to be immersed. She desperately wanted to be baptized but didn't
know how to do so with the monitoring bracelet on her ankle. She was
one of 1,247 on a weekend in May 2009 who were declaring Jesus as
Lord and Savior. We had preached the story of the Ethiopian eunuch
and asked the same simple question he asked Philip: "Here is water,
why not now?" We set up several baptisteries (a.k.a. swimming pools)
and tried to remove every excuse someone could make. We saw the
Holy Spirit move in a way we never imagined.

When the woman approached the baptistery, we assured her, "We've got this. We'll get the foot later." Our team picked her up and kept one foot hanging outside the pool. I still get goose bumps recounting that story.

I (Bart) was handing out towels that weekend, which was my last on the team before launching into the work of Intentional Churches. I saw small group members baptizing one another, parents baptizing kids, and a dude in Harley chaps fully immersed. "If I am going in," he said, "my leathers are going in with me. Jesus is getting *all* of me *right now!*"

This was one of the most beautiful moments I ever experienced as a pastor, and this certainly wasn't a human thing. It was a move of God. I felt so blessed to be in partnership with him in the miracle strategy called the local church. It was my own day of pentecost moment. I pray everyone in ministry gets a version of that moment.

But what, exactly, was my part? I had served on the executive leadership team for years in various roles. Not too long before this weekend baptism celebration, I assisted with the building of roads, bridges, and parking lots to give access to our property. While the building of roads and bridges doesn't sound like ministry or exactly what I was trained to lead, it was the imperative work of the next season. You never get a big baptism weekend like that if people can't get in and out of your church.

I can now trace back that incredible life-changing moment for me and others to the work that was done many years before. That work on some days felt like leading a church and on other days it felt human, boring, and administrative. Regardless, the work always embraced the leadership principles we laid out in chapter 1. We led as a team, had honest conversations, and sought to constantly improve for the sake of the gospel. It took rigorous evaluation and strong habits. We stayed aligned and focused on what was most important. It also required us to always keep in mind a common understanding of the key functions of the church and a dream of double impact.

But how do you know what to do on what day? How do you prepare today for the next season? How do you join God in releasing your church's potential? As pastors, we all want to see the growth and impact we read about in the book of Acts happen in our lifetimes, don't we? We want to see people saved daily!

It starts with a sincere and intimate partnership with the Almighty. Then we must be completely honest about our current state of affairs. We call it disciplined *discovery*. We have built the Great Commission Engine to lead us into this honest, fundamental discovery so we can ascend above our ministries and gain a collective, unified understanding of today's reality.

In this chapter we're going to be very practical. We are going to apply the three pistons and other components of the Great Commission Engine to your ministry. Instead of *teaching the purpose for each* (see chapter 3), we are going *to apply each to your church*. What must be true for each component to operate effectively? Remember, we must put modern skin on our two-thousand-year-old Acts 2 model.

IMPORTANT NOTE 1: If you haven't read chapter 2 about ChurchOS fundamentals, you need to go back and do so. We are about to embark on the phases of Intentional Growth Planning where our evaluation standards and methods will be used. They are simple to understand, but we won't be explaining them in detail again.

IMPORTANT NOTE 2: If you haven't read chapter 3 about the Great Commission Engine (Part 1), you need to go back and do so. This chapter stands on top of what we taught you there. You must understand the purposes of each component in order to honestly evaluate them.

WHAT MUST BE TRUE?

The Great Commission Engine is a simple analogy. Even more simply, as leaders we take action and make plans (programs,

ministries, strategies, services, systems) in each of the components
of the GCE to accomplish the Great Commission. For instance,
we hold weekend services, develop small group ministries, hold
Sunday school classes, and place volunteers in places of gifted
service—each fitting within the purview of one of the pistons. The
objectifying question for evaluation is this: *What must be true for this
component to fulfill its role in the model?* We are going to go piece
by piece through the GCE model and relate this to your ministry
in a simple way so you can move on to evaluate, rate, and diagnose
your core challenges in each area, namely, define today's reality
for your church.

A book could be (and many have been) written on each of these
components. Trust us, you do not need more than what we are going
to give you to begin the ChurchOS journey. Remember, we start with
self-assessment.

THE ONE

REMEMBER THE PURPOSE: **We are on mission with Christ. He said he came to
seek and save the lost. Then he told us to go make disciples, baptize, and
teach. Your Great Commission Engine revolves around the ONE.**

The ONE is a basic but profound concept. It refers to Luke 15
and the overt emphasis Jesus placed on the lost. If we could trace the
decline of impact in many churches to one thing, it would be the
erosion of this conviction and what it means to our church strategies
and plans. We are going to identify your ONE in chapter 6, but don't
skip ahead just yet. For now, think of a typical person or family in
your community who needs to know Christ. Let's start with some
basic self-evaluation.

HERE'S WHAT MUST BE TRUE

KNOW YOUR ONE: You must identify your ONE and know them intimately. You must know their name, the realities of their life in fullness, and have a measurable plan to judge how you are doing in reaching, connecting with, and making them into disciples on mission with you and Christ.

OWN YOUR ONE: Your church family must see their lives as spiritual outposts of the gospel. The ONE concept is both personal to them and corporately important to your church. Your church (the Ninety-Nine) is connected to many people who need to know Christ. They need to understand the power of prayer and invitation, both in terms of life with them and life at your church. And last, most people need to be trained how to start and have spiritual conversations that lead people to Christ.

BUILD A CHURCH FOR THE ONE: Your first filter in decision-making must be to have the ONE in mind. We will layer this onto the other components in the Great Commission Engine to show you what we mean. It's rare that we run into a church that doesn't have a heart to reach the lost, but upon close evaluation, the team realizes they aren't truly built for the ONE in all things.

CREATE AN IMBALANCE IN FAVOR OF THE ONE: Maybe the most important point we can make is that in order to achieve a balanced Great Commission activation outcome (keeping both more and better disciples in balance), we must imbalance our leadership toward the ONE. *We believe the necessary ratio of imbalance should be as great as 70/30 weighted toward the ONE.* Read that again. We must keep the passion for the ONE white-hot in our churches. Why? If we try to balance our leadership efforts, the gravitational force of the Ninety-Nine will turn your church inward. If you want an outcome ratio of 50/50 more and better disciples, you must imbalance your leadership to compensate for this gravitational force. Always remember, one of the best ways to grow your Ninety-Nine is be a church built for the ONE.

We have some theories on why churches turn inward and forget the ONE. Perhaps it's not that hard to understand. Folks who meet Jesus and then meet others who know Jesus love their new life in Christ. They love the fellowship and brotherhood that is found in these life-giving relationships. They want more for goodness' sake and almost can't get enough, so they slowly but surely lose sight of the lost and the ONE in their lives. Some even, slowly but surely, completely eliminate relationships with the lost in their lives.

Earlier in the book we called it the *pivot*. It's a hard pivot to make—to get someone of faith focused on others who need to know Christ and to see their life mission as now the shared mission of Christ and your church. Rick Warren nailed it at the beginning of *The Purpose Driven Life*: "It's not about you."[1] We must help people make this shift.

Have you felt it? Have you fought it? Fighting this pull is worth everything in your church. It will change everyone. And yes, there will be inevitable consequences. We don't take these thoughts and points of focus lightly. There are deep, eternal implications and potentially serious problems for your church.

At this moment we usually remind our teams that this is a strong leadership conversation. This (and other discussions) is a very internal-facing discussion that is going to lead to incredible conviction and perhaps courageous decisions that will shake things up. Remember, the Lord is with us on this mission, so do not fear but enter deeply into this evaluation.

Does this imbalanced focus on the ONE in your leadership mean we have to become an attractional church or adopt seeker-driven strategies? No. You are going to build a balanced church with the ONE always in mind. We've coined the term *ONE-aware* in all things.

We believe a focus on the ONE may be the greatest discipleship tool your church will ever see. Life in Christ, after all, is about a life-long journey of increasing surrender, and nothing drives surrender like a focus on others.

EVALUATION: THE ONE

YOUR OVERALL RATING

Here are some clarifying questions about the ONE—only evaluate this component. What is your rating? What is today's status? Use our red, yellow, and green rating system.

- Do we know our ONE?
- Do we intimately own the values of our ONE?
- Are we a church built ready for the ONE?
- Do we have the proper imbalance in our leadership to fight the inward pull of the Ninety-Nine?
- Are we focused inwardly? Really?
- How does this component rate in terms of driving Great Commission activation?
- How does this component rate in terms of helping us to double our kingdom impact?
- What is our overall rating?

IMPORTANT TIP: Wisdom has shown us to limit the discussion at this point and wait for the evaluation at the end of this chapter to discuss your individual rating rationale. If you are reading this as a team, allow everyone to rate your church based on minimum objective standards and then average the ratings. For example, we would average out four yellow ratings and three red ratings as an overall yellow rating for the purposes of discovery. It's also incredibly valuable to note and discuss the tension of one person voting green and another voting red for a category. You can use this tension to drive the discussion and refine the group's insight. Trust us on this! One more thing: Don't allow any hedging on the voting. Pick a color and stick with it until you have a chance to do more discovery work as a team.

Remember, we aren't yet drawing any conclusions! We are in a disciplined discovery phase. But as we go along, we might be getting hints at where God is leading us in the coming season.

PISTON #1 (CATALYTIC WEEKEND EXPERIENCE)

> REMEMBER THE PURPOSE: **Preaching saves people. If Christ is lifted up, he will draw people to him. With the Holy Spirit involved this is a powerful, catalytic, and spiritually explosive experience.**

Each of these components represent areas of action, tactics, programs, and strategies. In this case, it simply represents your weekend worship services. We have been gathering as a church for more than two thousand years in this way. This gathering, the *ecclesia*, delivers power to Great Commission activation in a way no other component can. Work occurs here that cannot be performed elsewhere. It is imperative we get it right and keep it healthy.

HERE'S WHAT MUST BE TRUE

PUT THE ONE-AWARE FILTER ON IT: We will say this at the outset of the evaluation of each component. It's why we established the ONE concept first. The crankshaft of the Great Commission Engine is the ONE. The engine revolves around the ONE that is lost, and remember, we must imbalance our effort to ensure that ONE-awareness is baked into the fiber of our church. This is certainly true in our weekend services. They can so quickly become insider focused and built for the Ninety-Nine and not the ONE.

MAKE IT MATTER: The weekend worship services are the spiritual starting point for so many people's spiritual journey. It is also the place where the Holy Spirit translates the gospel in a way that impacts everyone involved. The gospel should be preached and Christ lifted to his rightful position. For some reason, some churches diminish the importance of the weekend experience. You cannot forget its power. One church called it the Super Bowl—the biggest game of the year—and it's happening every week! Not a bad perspective in our view.

I (Doug) took my daughter to see the band Cold Play at the Rose

Bowl. It was an amazing experience and her first concert. Interestingly, the most poignant moment of the whole evening was when Chris Martin, the lead singer, sang "Amazing Grace" as a solo. When he started to sing, the revelry around us subsided, the whole bowl quieted. The audience was captivated and eventually joined in at the top of their lungs. It was the most powerful song of the evening. You see, foolish preaching saves people. Worship draws people in. His amazing grace means something to everyone when he is lifted up. Your worship services are more powerful if you think about it!

SEE WORSHIP AS A TOTAL EXPERIENCE: In this modern era, we must see our gatherings as experiential events where many things occur sequentially. Like links in a chain, if one of the moments is weak, the chain is at risk of giving way. Remember, we are keeping the ONE in mind.

Think of the experience through the eyes of the ONE. They heard about your church, hopefully from a friend. So they check out your website. What are they looking for? Maybe to see what you offer for their kids or maybe just to make sure you're not "weird." Are they able to easily find the website and read it clearly?

Once they've decided to visit, they get the kids up, dress everyone, and load into the car. They put your address in their map app, maneuver through traffic, spot your church sign, and turn in. How easily are they going to navigate your parking lot? Will they know which door to enter?

As they walk through the door of your church, they may be apprehensive, even intimidated. How are you structuring your church hallways and greeters to alleviate that?

Once in the worship center, they find a seat and get settled. Is the order of worship easy to follow? If they want to sing along, are the words clearly displayed? Do they get the whole experience, or is it confusing and disconnected?

After hearing your message, is the call clear? Do they know the next steps to take if they want to take a next step? Do they understand the meaning of words such as *salvation* and *baptism*?

Once you reverse engineer the experience, you see it's not really about pandering to a certain demographic. It's about being sensitive to the first visit of a spiritual seeker. How do they see the church that you've grown to see so well for so long? What changes need to take place to make life change more accessible? These are the real questions we ask when we focus our weekend worship on the ONE.

Here are the experiential linkages you are managing on the ONE's behalf:

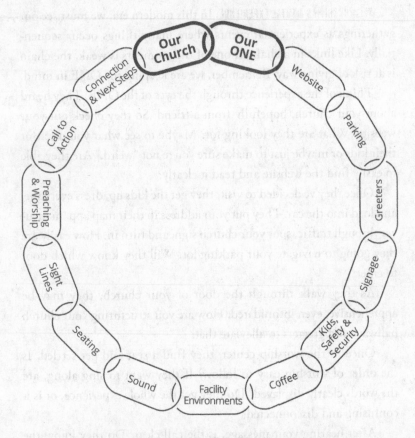

We call this the site-to-seat-to-street total experience.

We aren't going to belabor the point too much. Here's the simple truth: weaken any of those links and you lose the power, the right, and the ability to make an eternal connection to the ONE. Why are we prioritizing the ONE? Because a Ninety-Niner will have tons of grace for things that are experientially amiss. Bad coffee, intimidating greeters, smelly kid's areas, poor signage, irrelevant teaching, and long waits in the parking lot just don't matter as much to someone who has been at it awhile or been a part of your ministry for years. They've gotten to know you, and your good people, doggone it. Right?

We want to believe that the apostle Peter's thinking was similar in the temple courts. "Hi, I'm Peter, one of the pastors here today. We're glad you're here. Let us tell you about the greatest thing that's ever happened to mankind."

We're sort of joking, but in a church where "they added to their number daily," there had to be a prioritization toward the uninitiated. It was both part and parcel of the reason the movement grew so rapidly.

All of this matters. Why? Because eternity is at stake for the ONE. If the ONE cannot hear because they are distracted, they won't be moved by the Spirit or able to respond to the gospel. If they are intimidated and feel like outsiders, they won't come back next week. You may lose any chance to connect the ONE to us, Christ, and one another. It's that simple.

We believe the simple hindrances of packed parking lots, poor roads and signage, inhospitable environments, unsafe and stinky kid's areas, and cramped sanctuaries matter. Here are a couple of examples from our experience.

When we opened a new building at Central in Vegas, we were immediately assaulted by a terrible sewer gas smell. The best way to describe it was gag-inducing and repulsive, like the devil's bathroom probably smells. We knew for a fact that many people, especially our ONEs, would definitely rather stay in bed or watch an NFL game than come to church. The odor was so bad, even our Ninety-Niners were more interested in the Forty-Niners than church services. We chased the problem until we fixed it, but it took months. Our hearts were breaking because we knew for a fact the ONEs were choosing to not return. We knew it was happening and could trace attendance increases as we solved the problem.

I (Doug) had to solve a massive parking and traffic challenge as the average wait time to exit our lots grew to more than twenty minutes. We knew it would be a hindrance to our growth and ability to reach our ONEs if we did not solve the problem. Again, the ONEs lack the patience to wait twenty minutes just to get out of the church parking lot. The Ninety-Niners might wait or figure out a work-around. We knew the parking lot was going to take a big investment to solve. We started by buying a nearby property to expand our parking lot, and we worked with the city to add a new exit from our lot. It took money and time, but because of this simple but tough fix, we advanced to the next level of kingdom impact. All of these things matter.

You can try your best to live in denial. You can assume a miracle is coming or your church is the exception to the rule, but these things matter to the ONE. You can't break the rules for long and maintain momentum. No price is too great or honesty too rigorous to not do what it takes to remove the barriers to Piston 1 (Catalytic Weekend Experience) for the ONE.

EVALUATION: PISTON #1 (CATALYTIC WEEKEND EXPERIENCE)

YOUR OVERALL RATING

Here are some clarifying questions to consider what must be true about Piston 1 (Catalytic Weekend Experience)—only evaluate this component. What is your rating? What is today's status? Use our red, yellow, and green rating system.

- Do we make Piston 1 a priority?
- Do we see our services as a total experience for the ONE from site to street to seat to street?

- Are the experiential linkages in our weekend worship strong? Is there a weak link? (Think of each link in the experience.)
- Are we ONE-aware in all aspects of this component?
- How does this component rate in terms of driving Great Commission activation?
- How does this component rate in terms of helping us to double our kingdom impact?
- What is our overall rating?

Remember, we aren't yet drawing any conclusions! We are in a disciplined discovery phase. But as we go along, we might be getting hints at where God is leading us in the coming season.

PISTON #2 (LIFE-CHANGING RELATIONSHIPS)

> REMEMBER THE PURPOSE: The gospel and discipleship are relational topics. Disciples are best made in the context of relationships. The Holy Spirit works through relationships in a unique way. We are better together.

Each of these components represents a strategy or ministry we already have in our churches. Perhaps you have small groups, adult Bible fellowship groups, or Sunday school classes. You may also do other things to foster community and relationship building. We want you to have in mind the core program or strategy you use.

HERE'S WHAT MUST BE TRUE

PUT THE ONE-AWARE FILTER ON IT: If there is anywhere it's easy to forget the ONE, it's in this piston. Maybe it's because we typically view discipleship as something that happens after you're a Ninety-Niner and no longer the ONE. Make the effort to really keep the ONE in mind as you comb through these thoughts for evaluation. Connecting to Piston 2 (Life-Changing Relationships) is just as paramount for the ONE as it is for anyone in your ministry.

CREATE CIRCLES, NOT ONLY ROWS. ADD HEART TO HEAD: Classroom settings are needed. We must be taught the Word in order to grow. We attribute much of our understanding of the Bible to what we learned from teachers in classrooms, but the power of Piston 2 (Life-Changing Relationships) is released when we add a strong relationship component to it. This means you have to get out of rows (if you have them) and into circles, where the ONE and the Ninety-Niners can be face to face and get to know one another. You need intentional strategies to build Life-Changing Relationships. Relationships are fertile ground for growth, and Acts 2 was clear that hearts knitted together matter.

LEAVE OPEN CHAIRS: This may be one of the most glaring misses of many churches. The Piston 2 (Life-Changing Relationships) strategy isn't ready or equipped to receive someone new. We've seen Sunday school classes where the people's backs are to the door, and the door closes promptly at 10:00 A.M. (The ONE typically comes late.) Classes are situated along labyrinthine hallways, and if the ONE actually finds the right classroom, there's no place to sit because there are no extra chairs. Someone reasoned the same number of people come every week, so that's all the chairs they need.

Apply that example to your small groups. You must have an easy and natural method for connection or inclusion in the group, the groups need to be open to receiving new people, and they need to build Life-Changing Relationships. Going back to the ONE filter, is your Piston 2 (Life-Changing Relationships) strategy open to the ONE? In this arena, we typically build them for the Ninety-Nine, and they are committed to it and love it.

EVALUATION: PISTON #2 (LIFE-CHANGING RELATIONSHIPS)

YOUR OVERALL RATING

Here are some clarifying questions about what must be true about Piston 2 (Life-Changing Relationships)—only evaluate this component. What is your rating? What is today's status? Use our red, yellow, and green rating system.

- Is our Piston 2 (Life-Changing Relationships) strategy built in rows or circles?
- Do we have a proactive plan to build Life-Changing Relationships that we can measure and know are succeeding?
- Is connecting to our groups, Sunday school, missional communities, or ABF classes easy and natural for the ONE?
- Do we have fitting spans of care?
- Are we ONE-aware in all aspects of this component?
- How does this component rate in terms of driving Great Commission activation?
- How does this component rate in terms of helping us to double our kingdom impact?
- What is our overall rating?

Remember, we aren't yet drawing any conclusions! We are in a disciplined discovery phase. But as we go along, we might be getting hints at where God is leading us in the coming season.

PISTON #3 (SURRENDERED LIVING)

> REMEMBER THE PURPOSE: **God uses the application of the gospel to our lives to change us and make us more selfless over time. He uses this life-changing surrender to also build his church and accomplish his purposes.**

This component may be the hardest to understand, but it's crucial to Great Commission activation. We see Piston 3 (Surrendered Living) mismanaged and more poorly stewarded than any other component. It is a massive part of our churches, where the application of life change is going on through the power of the Holy Spirit, and our job is to harness that life change to grow the church. Here is what is included in this component:

- Generosity and stewardship
- Local and global outreach/missions
- Volunteering/serving
- Pastoral care and benevolence
- Relational evangelism

HERE'S WHAT MUST BE TRUE

PUT THE ONE-AWARE FILTER ON IT: This is a complex arena, as we mentioned earlier. These ministries hold great opportunities for the ONE. Places of meaningful contribution, a sense of purpose, and a place to belong can all be gained by getting plugged into Piston 3 (Surrendered Living). We believe it holds tremendous potential for onboarding and connecting the ONE, because of the deep desire for impact in the coming generations.

SEE THIS AS A TWO-SIDED CHALLENGE: You are responsible for both the call to action and the application of the action. This is one reason this piston is hard to manage. In the areas listed above, you must teach effectively about the biblical principles of each, but you must also provide pathways for involvement and related application. And you'd better have the ONE in mind at all times: what they need to know, where they can start in terms of taking action or applying your teaching, and how to ensure they keep growing.

THIS IS ALSO A TWO-WAY STREET: Through the energy generated by this piston, you can make an incredible impact in the world. (Remember our story about the emphasis of the generations on these components?) The mismanaged aspect of this piston often happens because of our inability to harness this energy and turn it into measurable Great Commission activation or impact across the Great Commission Engine. Simply put, what's occurring through this piston's energy should help us grow our church both in depth and breadth. Folding back this energy in this way can be difficult, but let's consider the following example.

Cumberland Community Church in Smyrna, Georgia, had a community garden they sponsored and tended alongside others from the community. Many of those serving from the community were ONEs who needed to know Christ. During one of our sessions, an elder told a fantastic story about pulling weeds next to the ONE. They struck up a spiritual conversation and made a connection. The elder invited the gentleman to his small group and he showed up! At group, they mentioned the weekend service and sitting together at the 9:00 A.M. service. He did that too! Through the power of invitation and some simple-smart intuition, this ONE was connecting with Cumberland, Christ, and others.

That's a great example of how to fold back the energy from this piston into the Great Commission Engine—the other ministries and kingdom efforts of your church. This will not happen without intentionality and creative effort. For instance, what Cumberland discovered incidentally could easily be fostered intentionally. Everyone serving at the community garden could be trained to strategically connect with others for the sake of the gospel.

PISTON #3 (SURRENDERED LIVING) COMES WITH SOME WARNINGS. We see many churches wanting to celebrate the great things that are happening as a result of Piston #3 (Surrendered Living). You can imagine the community impact, the money being given to foreign missions, and the celebration of high-per-capita giving. But none of these necessarily indicate healthy or Great Commission activation. We must be honest about what is going on. Here are some sobering truths.

WARNING #1: High-per-capita giving can be a sign a church has turned significantly inward. Sometimes the Ninety-Nine love the feast they are getting every week and are willing to pay anything to keep it coming. They love vicarious victories, but not necessarily those that come by getting their hands dirty in ministry. They don't actually own the ministry; they rent it and its wins.

WARNING #2: Community outreach and impact can be devoid of eternal impact. Incredible partnerships can be formed, many people impacted for good, but few, if any, are being impacted by the saving message of Jesus Christ. We've seen churches unwilling to put their name on these activities or describe their true motivations for fear of being selfish! We've seen preschool ministries where the mission was to reach people, but no one can tell you how or when it has happened. We've seen complete community outreach centers started that are starving the church budget, but they are hamstrung because they can't actually share the Good News because of restrictions with their community partnerships. You can imagine other scenarios. The ultimate purpose of these activities must be to partner with Christ on his mission to seek and save the lost.

WARNING #3: Big money going to foreign missions is a great thing. We are called to help spread the gospel to Jerusalem, Judea, Samaria, and the rest of the world. Such vision should be a part of every church's budget and operations. But we've seen more than one church die a slow death while celebrating its foreign victories. Millions of lost people within twenty miles of this church are going to die without Christ because the church's foreign work was hindering their local mission. We've seen churches celebrate 25 percent of their budget going to missions while fewer and fewer local people are being reached because of budget constraints. Eventually these churches are going to lose their permission and ability to impact anyone in Jerusalem and thus the rest of the world. If you lose sight of Jerusalem and Antioch, you are only one to two generations from death.

We know this can be dangerous ground to walk on, but we have some convictions about the matter. The early church was built to impact Jerusalem and then send missionaries. Sometimes we say, "This is a conversation about Jerusalem and Antioch first." But it's clear to us, and it should be to you as well: the home base must be guarded and tended just as we saw the apostles doing or we will lose everything. This means we have to face the honest truth about every aspect of our ministry—including Piston 3 and its potential pitfalls.

As Justin Teague, worship and communication pastor at Faithbridge in Spring, Texas, shared with us: "You can become disconnected from the Great Commission while still supporting missionaries. For some reason, you can find it easier to think about Samaria and the rest of the world and forget about Jerusalem and Judea."

EVALUATION: PISTON #3 (SURRENDERED LIVING)

YOUR OVERALL RATING

These clarifying questions about Piston 3 should be used to evaluate only this component. What is your rating? What is today's status? Use our red, yellow, and green rating system.

- How do we do at managing the two-sided challenge of Piston 3 (Surrendered Living)? Are we good at calling and teaching for action and then providing the appropriate next steps?
- Do we do a good job of releasing the impact that comes from our Piston 3 (Surrendered Living) strategies and also folding it back into our Great Commission Engine?
- Is Piston 3 prioritized to help us impact Jerusalem first so we can also make and steward impact to Judea, Samaria, and beyond?
- Are we ONE-aware in all aspects of this component?
- How does this component rate in terms of driving Great Commission activation?
- How does this component rate in terms of helping us to double our kingdom impact?
- What is our overall rating?

Remember, we aren't yet drawing any conclusions! We are in a disciplined discovery phase. But as we go along, we might be getting hints at where God is leading us in the coming season.

ENGAGEMENT PATHWAY

> REMEMBER THE PURPOSE: **Engaging with and connecting to the ONE is paramount. If we do not connect them to us, Christ, and one another, we aren't on mission with Christ.**

Most churches have a connection strategy of some type. If you do, we are going to lay out some objectifying principles for your strategy. We are also going to dive deeply into the design of an effective Engagement Pathway in chapter 7, but don't skip ahead. Consider what we describe here, and evaluate your current system.

HERE'S WHAT MUST BE TRUE

PUT THE ONE-AWARE FILTER ON IT: Your Engagement Pathway definitely should greatly impact your effort to reach the ONE. We want you to imagine the ONE has been driving by your church or visiting your website but cannot bring themselves to come through the door. The ONE is intimidated and potentially ashamed that the hurdle is just too great. But one day courage swells and the ONE decides to get out of the car and walk in. What happens next? We discussed the sequence earlier in this chapter, but here are some important basics.

BUILD IT WITH SLIPPERY, SIMPLE BABY STEPS: You need to envision making your Engagement Pathway as easy to enter as possible. This means you need to get into the life, heart, and head of the ONE. What is an intuitive first step they might take? Do you have an intuitive first step that works for connection?

You must break the path into simple steps that are sequentially connected and measured. For instance, perhaps your class to orient the

ONE to you and Christ is easily available and promoted. In fact, the normal four-hour class you've been promoting on Sunday evenings is now broken into four one-hour classes during or between the Sunday services. That's great simple-step building and thinking!

With the ONE in mind, you should break increasing commitments to you, Christ, and one another into finer, more doable, simple steps. This means you don't ask for a four-year commitment to serve in the nursery, you let the ONE get a taste of serving. You help the ONE find a place of gifted and meaningful service so they can participate in this life-changing work. The pathway needs to begin long before the ONE has decided to fully surrender to Christ.

MAKE IT RELATIONAL AS QUICKLY AS POSSIBLE: Gary McIntosh and Charles Arn gave us a stat that's still true today.[2] Once a person has made seven friendship connections at your church, they consider themselves a part of your church family. Convicting, huh? The question is, how quickly can you make those meaningful connections happen?

Most churches rely on a connection card for that first contact. That's fine, but is it adequate? When you consider the power of personal touch, filling out a card not only seems impersonal, it can be off-putting. We really need a new way to connect.

If you do not connect the ONE to you, Christ, and others, you cannot go on a spiritual journey together. If you don't go on the journey, you may lose the opportunity to make another disciple and more eternal ripples into heaven.

EVALUATION: ENGAGEMENT PATHWAY

YOUR OVERALL RATING

Here are some clarifying questions to consider about your Engagement Pathway. Evaluate only this component. What is your rating? What is today's status? Use our red, yellow, and green rating system.

- Is your Engagement Pathway built with slippery, simple baby steps?
- Do you have a measurable first step and sequential next steps that work well for the ONE?
- Do you get a loving person involved in connecting to the ONE early in the process?
- Are you ONE-aware in all aspects of this component and process?
- How does this component rate in terms of driving Great Commission activation?
- How does this component rate in terms of helping you to double your kingdom impact?
- What is our overall rating?

Remember, we aren't yet drawing any conclusions! We are in a disciplined discovery phase. But as we go along, we might be getting hints at where God is leading us in the coming season.

DEEPER EVALUATIONS: FOUR HELPFUL LISTS

You may need to refer back to chapter 2 for instructions. Four Helpful Lists is our go-to diagnostic tool when diving into the details about a topic. You need a frame for the discussion, and now you have five ratings collectively averaged by your team. Remember, there is great value in the tension between one voting red for a component and another voting green.

Now that you have a high-level rating, you will be discussing the next level of detail to support your vote. In this case, it's as simple as "Why did you rate this component as you did?" Any level of detail is pertinent. You will be asking the following four diagnostic questions about the five components of the Great Commission Engine and taking notes in the corresponding box or column:

- *What is right?* What can we amplify or leverage?
- *What is wrong?* What must be fixed?
- *What is missing?* What do we need to add?
- *What is confused?* What do we need to clarify?

For example, let's use Piston #1 (Catalytic Weekend Experience). Here are some next-level potential comments:

- RIGHT: "We've upgraded our video and sound systems." The note in the box or column could read "Upgraded AVL Systems."
- WRONG: "Our stage communication is cluttered and confusing to the ONE." The note in the box or column could read "Confusing platform communications."
- MISSING: "Signage from the street to the seat, especially for the ONE." The note in the box or column could read "Signage for the ONE."
- CONFUSED: "Who is in charge of recruiting and placing ushers and greeters?" The note in the box or column could read "First impressions leadership."

Fill each box and complete a thorough review of each component of the Great Commission Engine.

Here are some additional helpful tips:

- You can use the four-box design as we have represented it in chapter 2 on a piece of paper or a whiteboard, or you can create four columns on a whiteboard, or with two sheets of easel paper taped together, side-by-side.
- You can go component by component through the Great Commission Engine or open up the whole model for comments. We recommend you open the discussion to all four lists at once—any comment in any column is valid.
- Limit your discussion time to a few items for each component

and let the borders or space provided be a limiting factor. It's
rare you can't get the primary issues listed within one or two
hours. You will also get faster at this the more you use this and
the other tools.

- Once complete, circle one or two items in each box or column
that seem to rise above the others in terms of importance. You
can achieve this through discussion, or give each person an
equal number of votes per box or column and watch the team's
collective wisdom emerge.

- As your team votes, remember the evaluation criteria and methods from chapter 2. The votes are always about prioritizing the
ends of Great Commission activation and double kingdom
impact.

FINAL THOUGHTS

You made it! We are proud of you for digging in and beginning the
journey of self-discovery through disciplined discovery. It's not easy.
We typically want to jump ahead and solve problems as soon as we
see them. This is the nature of our Western minds and general sense
of urgency. You will be rewarded for your patience.

But we aren't drawing conclusions. This is still a phase of
disciplined discovery. Still, you might be getting hints at where God
is leading you.

Intentional Churches understand the biblical fundamentals of the
Great Commission and the strategies to accomplish it. They know
how to be rigorously honest but patient in discovering the truth of
their current situation. They don't jump to action before they have
clarity and alignment as a team.

Let's change angles and do some more disciplined discovery.

CHURCH OR THIRD WORLD AIRPORT?

FIRST BAPTIST CHURCH—ORLANDO, FLORIDA

Matthew Robinson

Beverly serves on our guest services team. She started weeping the first time she was invited to the training event at which we described our ONE and the Great Commission Engine and how it impacts our weekend experiences. She was crying because she saw firsthand what the church's inattention to a focus on the ONE had caused. A frustrated non-English-speaking family came through our doors and then turned and walked away and drove home because they could not navigate everything at our church.

We recognized we didn't want that to be Beverly's volunteer story or any guest's story ever again. Just putting some attention, time, and energy into making the experience better can make such a difference.

Our ONE is named Stephen. He is thirty-five years old with a child and a woman he loves but hasn't married. He moved here from Brazil and has been here for twenty years. He is fluent in two languages and spends his life chasing ambition, but he has some notion of solid moral values and is coming back to church for his child, more than anything else.

Through our Intentional Growth Plan, we recognized that the first-time guest process was horrific. Stephen would park, spend fifteen minutes walking in, followed by another fifteen minutes of checking in his child. He arrived at church thinking he had plenty of time, but he would get into the service feeling exhausted and frustrated. Meanwhile, staffers would look at their watches and say to themselves, "Didn't this guy know this started twenty minutes ago?" Truth is, Stephen exited the interstate with ten minutes to spare, thinking he'd be fine.

We have begun transforming our campus and taking care of the low-hanging fruit. We are removing some of the obstacles to the weekend experience and making our campus less like a Third World airport. From the changes we have made thus far, we are seeing an increase in the retention of visitors.

STRUCTURING AROUND THE ENGINE

CENTER POINTE CHRISTIAN CHURCH—CINCINNATI, OHIO

Steve Poston

We are a thirty-year-old church with five senior pastors. We would go through new visions or focuses, lean outward, then settle, and slowly lean inward again. Since 2015, we've been working through the ChurchOS constructs. We've leaned into the Great Commission Engine to the point we have structured our staff in adult ministries as such, keeping us balanced and focused. We have a creative arts pastor who is focused on Piston 1 (Catalytic Weekend Gathering). We have a groups pastor focused on Piston 2 (Life-Changing Relationships) and a missions pastor leading Piston 3 (Surrendered Living). Our connections pastor is rooted in the Engagement Pathway and simple-step process, especially at the top half of the engine, between weekend gathering and rich community. Our whole team is focusing our bias on the ONE—the lost. This has helped us organize and focus our staffing consistently.

The Great Commission Engine is anchored to the Father's heart for lost people. As an executive pastor of adult ministries, the GCE helps me narrow my focus and spend as much time working *on* the organization rather than *in* the organization. It helps me stay simplified and at the same time elevated to the right level of leadership.

For more stories and case studies, please visit
www.intentionalchurches.com.

FIVE

SQUATTERS, CUL-DE-SACS, AND BUFFETS

> For everything there is a season,
>> a time for every activity under heaven.
>> A time to be born and a time to die.
>> A time to plant and a time to harvest.
>> A time to kill and a time to heal.
>> A time to tear down and a time to build up. . . .
>
>> A time to search and a time to quit searching.
>> A time to keep and a time to throw away.
>> A time to tear and a time to mend.
>> A time to be quiet and a time to speak.
>
> —ECCLESIASTES 3:1–3, 6–7

During the 2008–9 economic recession, an issue with squatters emerged in our hometown of Las Vegas. People were moving into abandoned homes, usually foreclosures, and making them their own. They had no concern for the maintenance of the home or the well-being of their communities and became incredibly difficult to evict.

One of the best places to find squatters in Las Vegas were the cul-de-sacs. We all like them. They are safe places to live, and if you find one with nice neighbors, you want to live there for a long time. Some people invite others into their cul-de-sac and develop deep bonds. They leave occasionally to see the outside world, but it's on their terms and they always return home. There is no through traffic, and they like it that way.

Since we're on the subject, we want to share one more feature of our hometown that is relevant, and that's our great buffets. We're sure you've enjoyed a buffet or two in your time, especially on a Sunday after church. You'll forgive us for saying this as hometown natives, but Las Vegas buffets are *unrivaled*. You've never seen anything like them! Lines stretching for what seems like miles. Three hundred dishes made fresh hourly, a plethora of desserts, gelato bars, and cots for napping. There are dozens of buffets to choose from. It's the essence of over-indulgence and too many choices.

So why talk about squatters, cul-de-sacs, and buffets? Maybe you can spot the analogies in ministry.

Some of our ministries and programs are occupied by squatters. The telltale signs are a lack of big-picture ownership or true care for their church community. They're only there for themselves and usually deflect every challenge that comes their way.

Cul-de-sacs in the church are similar to dead-end ministries that are no longer effective but are still hanging around. You get the picture. Cul-de-sacs should be challenged too. Can we open up the street and get some through traffic? Can you come see us more often?

Buffets are those long stretches of ministry upon ministry, each claiming they are the most important yet none living up to expectations. They take a lot to keep going, with constant upkeep, and the church is left with depleted resources and few strategically fed.

There is a legacy strategy of the church-growth era dating back some thirty or forty years, but still alive today, that has created a similar effect in churches. This is the belief of some experts, consultants, and church leaders that more and more programs are a way to grow the impact of the local church. I (Bart) remember hearing teaching sessions on the benefits of multiple specialty programs in the church. It was espoused as one of the benefits of the megachurch. For non-megachurches, it could create entry points, or on-ramps, into life in the church. Some leaders and churches went so far as to say it was God's strategy to grow the church. If you had a dream and a calling from God, they would get behind it and call it a ministry of the church.

Not long ago, we launched the ChurchOS journey at a midwestern church. A kind, godly church elder handed us a copy of untouchable topics prior to our first two-day session with the leadership team. He wasn't trying to warn us about the off-limit topics because he was a controlling leader. He was a kind leader trying to protect us and his church. He knew some topics were simply so sensitive they might derail our time with the team.

Among the list was a drive-through nativity that had been around for years. Thousands of cars made their way to the church every Christmas to see the wonderful live-action scene. But the church had little concrete evidence the Great Commission was activated in any way because of the event. Furthermore, the church was about to spend more than $100,000 on a space to store the components of the nativity scene while struggling to fund other important ministry work. This is a concrete example of a strategy gone awry. The nativity was a buffet item with a big commitment. It was a cul-de-sac with no access to the Great Commission. Squatters lived there and refused to move.

Herein lies an important truth: yesterday's solutions always create tomorrow's problems, and today's innovations become tomorrow's challenges. This is definitely true with the programmatic emphasis in our churches. This is why we must develop routine methods of rigorous, honest evaluation, because strategies don't work forever. Nothing should be sacred—except the gospel—when it comes to Great Commission activation.

Well-meaning efforts to grow the church's impact through multiple programs have led to a plethora of issues. We've seen it. We could give you example after example. One church had more than

220 programs that were strangling the church's vision and Great Commission activation. Here are a few unintended consequences:

- Ineffective legacy ministries with little to no Great Commission activation sap resources.
- Consumer Christians who love and enjoy the ministry or program of which they are part have no thought about any others, especially the ONE. They come to the buffet only to consume.
- Ministry bloat leads to big buildings, large staffs, and unwieldy if not unsustainable budgets.
- Confusion for the ONE. "Where do I start?" "What's my next step?"
- Silver-bullet thinking equals the answer that more programs must be the answer. What's the next one that will attract more people and grow this church?

These are just a few of the issues that squatters, cul-de-sacs, and ministry buffets can create. In some churches, it is the number-one challenge to spiritual movement and development. The confusion for the ONE, strangled resources, and ensconced/unchallenged commitments by the consuming Ninety-Nine are hard to overcome. These programs are stagnant holding ponds where sacred cows live and people go to die!

WHY DOES THIS MATTER?

This matters because you are a steward of the church, and you need to make the most of what you've been given. Prioritization may be the paramount challenge of church leaders over time. What is most important on any given day can be difficult to discern. As a steward of Christ's church, you want to make sure every ounce of energy, every cent of every dollar, and every second of every minute is spent as wisely as possible. Intentional Churches and Intentional Leaders know how to *prioritize*.

This means you need (or soon will need) a new strategy for addressing old systems and languishing effectiveness. You need a method to make sense of the ministry buffet and to clear up the challenge of squatters in your cul-de-sacs. First, let's take a cue from a certain business strategy we believe translates well and brings conviction when it comes to resources.

Does it ever feel like you don't have enough? You spend every penny you have as wisely as possible, but you continually face budget shortfalls. At the end of each day there's always work left undone. With only 20 percent of the people doing 80 percent of the work, you are constantly looking for more help. The reality is church leadership is a zero-sum, limited resource proposition.

What do we mean by zero-sum? It means that as leaders we must realize that when we invest in one place, we must divest from somewhere else. Before you start something new, you need to stop something old. If you want to deploy a new ministry strategy because you just came back from an incredible leadership conference, there will be a price to pay. Another way to say that is no effort or output goes without input, and that input must be measured against all the other inputs already demanding your efforts. It's a two-column universe of debits and credits.

As leaders, we have four commodities at our disposal: time, effort, money, and attention. Yes, we firmly believe attention is the fourth commodity we use to lead our church. Getting people's attention is tough, and when you have it, you had better use it wisely! Do we need to talk about screens, screens, and more screens in front of people?

Hear us on this: God is the only source of new energy in the universe. God can choose to infuse new spiritual resources into the system anywhere and at any time he chooses. He can do immeasurably more than we hope, dream, or count on. But as we wait for his supernatural breakthrough, we must work within the limitations we have.

Thus, one of our primary jobs as church leaders is to navigate the dicey topic of prioritization. What can go away? What can wait? What's next? These are really big questions! ChurchOS is built to help you prioritize your leadership effort and, in doing so, let you downgrade good things so the best things get your attention.

You could list everything you and your church, leaders, volunteers, and the rest put your efforts into. It will be a long list. Some things will be in better shape in terms of Great Commission activation and some things will lag behind. A legacy effort or two probably need to go away and a couple of others need to be overhauled and rebuilt.

You are in a limited-resource environment and you must prioritize. Here are two ideas that will help. Your team needs to understand these foundational thoughts to ChurchOS. Stay with us, because we are going to do some more evaluation at the end of this chapter.

THE RELATIONAL REACH ZONE

The concept is simple but profound and pivotal. The spreading of the gospel happens primarily through relationships—those within your direct sphere of influence. These relationships fit into the categories of friends, family, colleagues, and coworkers. If we want to spread the gospel and double our kingdom impact, the future frontier of that expansion lies within the relationships of the people who call your church home. Each of these followers of Christ are points of gospel light surrounding your ministry. Furthermore, this relationship network is central to the development of your Ninety-Nine as they begin to see it as a personal opportunity to spread the gospel. This potential reach zone has two important dimensions to it: the physical and the spiritual, with some important math to consider.

YOUR LOCATION MATTERS

You are trying to expand the kingdom footprint of gospel impact primarily in the spiritual realm, but there is a physical reality to this expansion, and it's tied to your Great Commission Engine. Think about it. How far will people drive to your Catalytic Weekend

Experience (Piston 1)? In some places, no more than twenty minutes. In other places, like Southern California, where heavy traffic is a daily reality, the drive time could be longer. But you know your context best. So how far will your neighbors drive to go to a church they've never been to? The truth is, if the ONE cannot or will not intersect with your catalytic teaching and worship, how will they connect to you through your Engagement Pathway?

On a map, draw a circle around your church the distance you think most people are willing to drive. That's your *Relational Reach Zone*. That's your Jerusalem. That's the area where you will have the greatest impact. Now, what are you doing to reach them? What is the main demographic, the level of education, their interests and likes, and how are you leveraging that to keep your on-ramp as accessible as possible?

Think about the physical aspects of Pistons 2 (Life-Changing Relationships) and 3 (Surrendered Living) in the Great Commission Engine. Almost always there is a physical dimension to your ministry strategies that will be hindered if you don't pay close attention to the physical dynamics of your Relational Reach Zone. Small groups, outreach events, and your church family inviting their friends to church all revolve around the physical aspects of your church.

YOUR SPIRITUAL FOOTPRINT MATTERS MORE

From God's vantage point, he could easily explain where the spiritual footprint of impact lies for your church. There are things happening you cannot see with your physical eyes, but that does not make them less important. In fact, they are the most important aspect of your ministry. It is contained in the relational network of the people connected to your church.

The people who call your church home intersect with so many other people throughout the week, more than come to your weekend service. And when they come into contact with them, there is a chance for a spiritual connection. It could be a conversation that opens the way to discuss faith, a need that can be prayed about, or a decision about following Jesus that can be made. We call these *gospel impact opportunities*. Each of your people represent the total sum of your church's spiritual reach through these opportunities.

Yes, this is somewhat physical in nature, but the more important dynamic is the spiritual one. In this age of digital relationships, this footprint could have a virtual aspect to it as well. Think about it. (We wonder if digital relationships are true relationships, but we trust God to lead us into this frontier in the coming years.)

Thus, with the physical and spiritual dynamics in mind, here are some important realizations.

> YOUR CHURCH HAS HAD AND IS HAVING MORE IMPACT THAN YOU LIKELY KNOW. Only in heaven will you know the eternal, positive kingdom ripple effect of your church. What a glorious day that will be! It's so easy to focus on the faces you see every day, but you have no idea how a single sermon or catalytic moment causes a ripple all the way into eternity. You underestimate the potential impact you could be having as well. (We'll get to the math in a moment.)
>
> THERE IS NO SUCH THING AS CHURCH COMPETITION. If there is one thing we've had enough of in our work with hundreds of churches and pastors, it's hearing the moaning and groaning about the other churches within your reach zone. It may be the church down the street that seems to have more cars in the parking lot than your church. Or it may be the rumor you heard of a megachurch satellite campus opening across town. The complaints usually come from a place of fear that you'll lose your people to these other churches.

We understand the difficulty of losing members and regular attenders to other churches. This can be painful and poignant, especially when they are close friends. Just remember, if you are getting serious about implementing something like ChurchOS, with a hyper-focus on the ONE, you will likely lose some people, but you will be rewarded with a church family more committed to you and on fire for Jesus' mission than you can imagine.

You see, the ONE doesn't church shop. The ONE is in relationship with someone from your church or a friend of a friend, and that means your potential for reach is unique. Church members from other churches are the ones usually shopping for a new church. If someone or a family from another church wants to connect to yours and join the mission, that's wonderful. Conversely, if someone from your church wants to find another church, that's okay too. When you are running ChurchOS, more times than not, you will lose church members who want to act more like consumers than contributors. If you do lose people, you want it to be for the right reasons. When you are on mission with Jesus, not everyone will follow.

Tates Creek Road in Lexington, Kentucky, is the site of three megachurches whose properties nearly abut one another side by side. Within the span of about a mile, you have a nondenominational church, a Baptist church, and a United Methodist church. Each has strong leadership and a unique vision and heritage. On the one hand, they could view each other as competition, each one vying for customers. On the other hand, they could see their three churches as a triple outpost of the gospel, each with a unique spiritual footprint. Thus they are three churches with more opportunity for unique kingdom impact than they might have dreamed.

We believe *there is no such thing as church competition*. No one church can do it all, but every church can do its part, and when each church does its part, they all work together to grow God's kingdom.

THE MATH MATTERS TOO

There is some math to the Relational Reach Zone that you must understand in order to create the right priorities. We understand math may not be your thing, but we promise it matters.

So here's the mathematical reality.

You likely know off the top of your head your church's average weekend attendance. We call this your AWA. For the sake of this exercise, let's say your AWA is 500, adults and kids included. (People usually ask us how to count, and we say counting everyone once is a good start!) However you count attendance, it's important you count consistently so you can establish an accurate baseline for planning.

Next, in our work with hundreds of churches, we have studied the frequency of church attendance among those that call a church home. This study has shown us that the average is typically between 1.2 and 2.0 times per month. Which means if you are a typical church with an AWA of 500, you can multiply that by 3 (frequency multiplier) to see how many regular attenders are within the larger purview of your leadership and shepherding. Fifteen hundred (1500) are likely looking to your church for spiritual guidance and could call your church home. You are a megachurch and may not have known it—until now!

We are asked if this holds true across denominations, types, and sizes of churches. Our experience has shown us it does. We are asked how to verify this number or frequency of attendance. Our best advice is to study your children's ministry check-in numbers over a period of time. (Hopefully, you have a check-in system.) You will learn a lot. For instance, for one quarter you could note the families that have checked-in their children and how frequently they have done so. With a little creativity, your team could start to zero in on how frequently people are attending your church. You will develop your own AWA frequency multiplier. Until then, let's guess it's somewhere around three.

Now, here's some additional math. Let's say you are a church with 1,500 that call you home at some level of commitment and are on mission with you. The most important math of the Relational Reach Zone may be found by multiplying the spiritual-relational gospel impact opportunity within the networks of those people. For purposes of illustration, let's say it's 10 gospel impact opportunities. That's a total of 15,000 opportunities in a church of 500. Let's say it's 20 (we think it's typically more!). That's a total of 30,000 opportunities. Do you get the picture? There's almost always more spiritual opportunity than you realize, and your church is bigger than you think. This is why we don't let any church of any size off the hook when it comes to thinking about and planning for double kingdom impact!

Here are the simple formulas described above:

AWA (average weekend/worship attendance) = _____

AWA x frequency multiplier = actual size

actual size x average gospel opportunities = total opportunities!

Our advice? Dream big! Keep this math in mind as we continue. Intentional Churches have a handle on the real math of the Relational Reach Zone and the evangelistic potential of their church.

SPIRITUAL MOVEMENT HAWKS

Here is the second key concept that is going to lead to better prioritization. It will also inform your ministry buffet clean up as well as clearing out the squatters in your cul-de-sacs.

As church leaders, we must develop a keen eye and a keen sense for when our church is stagnating. Stagnation is the enemy of a growing local church. The big idea of church is spiritual development. We are helping people far from God connect to us, him, and others in order to go on a lifelong journey of increasing commitment. That's it. Therefore, we must become the sworn enemy of spiritual stagnation.

Here is a simple paradigm we developed at Central Church, adapted from the classic Engel scale.[1] It really helps us keep this concept in proper perspective:

WE DO THIS AND ONLY THIS!

-5 ————————→ Jesus ————————→ +5

The numbers are arbitrary, but the point is clear. We help people far from God meet Jesus and grow up in him. Our job is not to save them but to help them move from -5 to +5 and beyond! We do this by leveraging our gospel opportunities.

In 2011, Greg Hawkins and Cally Parkinson's book *Move: What 1,000 Churches Reveal About Spiritual Growth* came along and gave us some language for this by categorizing the developmental stages as (1) searching for God, (2) exploring Christ, (3) growing in Christ, (4) close to Christ, and (5) Christ-centered.[2] You likely have people at all stages in your church. The movement through these stages is marked by increasing surrender to the lordship of Christ and the adoption of his mission as ours. One of your top jobs as a church leader is to foster and facilitate this movement. You are to help everyone develop as a follower of Christ and never stop moving toward Christ-centeredness.

This concept can be simple and helpful, but please don't misunderstand; spiritual development is not a linear process and it does not end. If you think of it this way, you are in danger of creating Christian consumers with more and more distance from the ONE. This continuum, however, never puts more space between you and the ONE but actually brings you closer to Christ's mission of seeking and saving the ONE. The more Christ-centered you become, the more you realize you are walking alongside those who are far from God and helping them along the same journey you are taking.

So how do you become a spiritual movement hawk? Here are some simple ideas.

STEP THINKING AND DESIGN. Canyon Ridge Church in Las Vegas has developed a saying that has become the mantra for their ministry: "We build next steps for everyone and first steps for their friends." Step thinking is part art, part science. We've been thinking about it ever since Andy Stanley wrote, "Practice 2: Think Steps Not Programs," in *7 Practices of Effective Ministry*.[3] This is especially true for the ONE, who definitely thinks and acts in steps.

Every ministry or subministry should be challenged with these questions: From where? While here? On the way to where? It has to be ingrained in the leadership to be building and designing ministry that takes a person (preferably the ONE) *from somewhere,* develops them *while there,* and is always thinking about how to foster and facilitate the next step *from there.* Does that make sense?

- Church softball isn't a means unto itself; it's a way to connect a new player to existing players, get them into community, and challenge them to serve or to be a better dad.
- Serving in the nursery once a month isn't just about making sure diapers are changed; it's about connecting with others and growing into a leader in a ministry area.
- Women's Bible study isn't about just putting your head into the Word; it's about bringing a new friend you met at work, connecting her with other like-minded women, finding a place of meaningful contribution, and seeing her come to Christ and bring her family to church.

You can retool your ministries with step thinking and design. Every leader must learn to ask *from where, while here,* and *on the way to where.* It's all about movement!

CLEANING UP AND CLEARING OUT

We are in the final stages of discovery, ascending above the battlefield as a team. We are going to walk you through some practical steps that could directly impact your Intentional Growth Plan. As we do, remember the key concepts we laid out in the Relational Reach Zone and the math and how to be a spiritual movement hawk.

FIRST, LET'S CHART THE BUFFET

This is such a big issue, we want to give you a tool to help you list, highlight, and sort through your ministry buffet. If the buffet is not a challenge now, count your blessings and you can save it for another day! Not only will this help you sort out your ministry programs, it will also reinforce some key thinking of ChurchOS. Again, we owe our friends at the Paterson Center for

CHART THE BUFFET

L — Life Change & Double Impact — H

H (Resources)	Foolish:	Bold:
	• • • •	• • • •
L (Resources)	Safe:	Gold:
	• • •	• • • •

inspiring this chart and our thinking. Tom Paterson developed similar tools to process decisions about programs and strategies wisely.

Here are the simple instructions:

- Draw this chart on a piece of paper or on a whiteboard.
- The top range of the chart represents life change and double kingdom impact—Great Commission activation.
- The range to the left measures the resources used to execute the program or strategy—time, effort, money, and attention. (Remember the zero-sum idea at the beginning of this chapter.)
- Take out a list of your ministry programs, strategies, and efforts. If one gets any resources at all, it's a candidate for the chart!
- Don't initially label the chart blocks as foolish, bold, gold, and safe, especially if you are doing this exercise with a larger group. You can label the quadrants at or near the end.

- Talk through each program, strategy, etc. The first discussion should be about the honest impact of a program (the top range), and then talk about the resources it requires (the range to the left).
- List the ministries in the quadrant where they best fit, and then prioritize the most foolish, boldest, safest, and gold-est.
- You can use the same discussion or voting method you used in chapter 4 to lock down the top items in each list. Here are some clarifying questions for the voting: What's the most foolish? What's the boldest? What's the safest? Where is the gold?
- Here is the next level of questions for each category:
  - Foolish: Should we stop or pause this?
  - Bold: How do we prioritize this?
  - Safe: Is this a sacred cow or just for the Ninety-Nine?
  - Gold: How do we accelerate or elevate this?
- Finally, discuss what this one chart is saying to you as a team.

If you want to ignite your Relational Reach Zone and fight spiritual stagnation as a spiritual movement hawk, you must set some priorities. Here are the three resource priorities of Intentional Churches who install and run ChurchOS.

RESOURCE PRIORITY #1: RELATIONAL EVANGELISM

Without a relational connection, no amount of advertising, branding, event-focused programming, or community involvement will get people to become followers of Jesus. That's a fact. Any evangelism efforts must be coordinated with the existing relationships your people have with those in your reach zone. All else may well be wasted effort.

The problem is not our focus but our follow-through. Recent data from the Barna Group suggest a smaller percentage than ever before in the church view personal evangelism as important. They report almost two out of five practicing Christians say they have no non-Christian friends or family members, and nearly half of millennial practicing Christians say it is wrong to evangelize![4] That means we are not engaging our world around us as we should. A very large component of your church's effectiveness is going untapped.

The reasons are many. For one, people feel a lot less confident in sharing their faith. With the rise of biblical illiteracy, fewer believers are able to tell someone the basics of what they believe or even encourage another person to believe the same! Couple that with a nonchalant attitude toward church attendance, and more Christians are sitting on the sidelines than ever before.

Another factor seems to be fear. In our oversensitive culture, we are afraid of offending someone else. What if we say the truth in a way that is misconstrued as offensive? The reality is, the truth can be offending. Many times in his ministry, Jesus upset those who were listening to him. Even Peter remarked that Paul's teachings were difficult to take (2 Peter 3:16). We cannot allow the sensitivities of our audience's emotions to override the seriousness of our message.

The Bible is clear about what it takes to know Jesus: "Everyone who calls on the name of the LORD will be saved" (Rom. 10:13). The goal of the Great Commission Engine is to help you know how to make more and better disciples that increasingly surrender to Christ for life. Salvation is and always has been the first deciding step in that journey: to call on his name and be saved.

The problem we face today is clear. This cannot happen if the church is sitting on the sidelines and passively hoping for it. We'll let Paul's words in the next verse speak loud and clear for us: "But how can they call on him to save them unless they believe in him? And how can they believe in him if they have never heard about him? And how can they hear about him unless someone tells them?" (v. 14).

What will it take for your people to get engaged in relational evangelism? Do they understand their role in disciple making? Are they aware of the stakes? Are they prepared for the challenge? Are they bold enough to begin engaging their friends, neighbors, and family in spiritual conversations to help them move further into knowing Jesus? These are the beginning questions of any evaluation.

So how are you doing on Resource Priority 1 (Relational Evangelism)? Use our red, yellow, and green rating system and discuss your ratings as a team.

RESOURCE PRIORITY #2: CATALYTIC WEEKEND EXPERIENCE

Your weekend worship experience is the starting point for the spiritual journey for so many. It's also the place the Holy Spirit speaks to us in a corporate setting. In fact, it's the one time each week you have the heaviest hand in creating a powerful movement for your Great Commission Engine.

Think of all the things that go into it. Preparing for your weekend worship experience and executing it well takes up a large percentage of your time and energy. Now, divide that weekend service into its component parts. There are the greeters who help people navigate from the parking lot to a seat in the worship center. There are the volunteers in each age-specific ministry who take care of children during worship but also help them become followers of Jesus. Then there's the worship itself, involving musicians, vocalists, sound technicians, light and camera operators, and even video techs. Behind them may be a creative department who develops the look and feel of the entire service. Finally, as the main communicator, you are tasked with sharing the Word of God in a compelling manner.

Each of these parts usually turns independently of each other. At the top is the lead pastor who tries to make sure each is running smoothly and effectively. Often that just means keeping them out of each other's way. But what if all these components worked together? As the Great Commission Engine is made up of three pistons that help the next with each turn, your weekend service can be viewed the same way.

What is it you hope to accomplish each weekend? In their book *The Power of Moments*, Chip and Dan Heath talk about coming up with a singular focus.[5] Think about your last vacation. What is it you remember about it? Doubtfully it's the beginning or the end. There are large parts in the middle you likely skip over. For instance, when you think back to a family visit to Disneyland, are the long lines what come to mind or the fun you had on the rides? Of course, it's those moments of great joy and fun! It's the same with your worship service. People will remember the moments.

The Heaths call such moments "short experiences that are both memorable and meaningful." They stick with you. You recall them easily. They are impactful and, in fact, life changing. When viewed through the lens of your church, your weekend worship service is an opportunity to create moments that can lead to real life change.

So back to that previous question, what do you hope to accomplish each weekend? A better way to ask it is, what moment do you want to create for the ONE? It can be a stirring response time at the altar. It can be a decision-making moment when people give their hearts to Jesus. It can be a creative element that hammers home the importance of your vision. Whatever it is, it must align with the intent of a catalytic worship experience, namely, to connect people to God.

Now, if you have one or two moments that you hope to create each week, what if your whole team were on board? What if the greeters were aware of the exact moment you were going to push for a response? They would be primed to keep distractions to a minimum. What if your children's ministries knew what was happening in the worship center? They would be ready to answer questions from parents later or even create a similar experience for the kids. What if your worship team knew where you were going? They could shape the song list to prime the hearts of hearers to be ready to receive. It's that simple! Having a singular goal of creating a memorable and meaningful moment can be the deciding factor in whether your service is successful or not.

So how are you doing on Resource Priority 2 (Catalytic Weekend Experience)? Use our red, yellow, and green rating system and discuss your ratings as a team.

RESOURCE PRIORITY #3: STRATEGIC COMMUNICATION

Hopefully you are following along here. These priorities are intended to create momentum and clean things up, especially when it comes to reaching and moving the ONE. If the ONE has come through the door because of a relational invite and now been moved poignantly through your Catalytic Weekend Experience, it's time to communicate well about what to do next. Here are some thoughts that might help you strategically communicate the next step.

Most churches say too many things to their church family at once. This is especially true of worship services. People are simply overloaded with a plethora of communication, both from the stage and in print. It's not too different from receiving a Valpak in the mail. (Do you know what that is? It's a package with about a hundred different advertisements and coupons, most of which—if not all of them—will be irrelevant to you. Most people don't even open it and just toss it in the trash.) That's not too different from what happens when you overcommunicate; people's ears just toss it all out. You can say everything to everyone and have *no one* hear *anything*.

One of the unintended consequences of overcommunication is the ministry buffet mentality. If your bulletin or program looks like a Cheesecake Factory menu, you are sending the message you have something available for every appetite in the room. You are fostering a consumeristic mentality. Furthermore, you are making it difficult for the ONE to know what to do next or how to engage you.

Believe it or not, you can grow a church at pace and only drive one, two, or three calls to action from the pulpit or platform. We challenge you to think about how you can minimize your stage promotions and maximize your call to action. If you use your ONE-aware filter, it will help as well. What does the ONE need to hear this week, every week? Amazingly, you will also connect many of your disconnected Ninety-Nine at the same time as the ONE.

Churches that are running ChurchOS learn how to say less and yet create more movement. Remember, you are a spiritual movement hawk! A good example of the calls to action would be (1) a decision for Christ, (2) a major all-church event (like Easter), (3) next steps for the ONE, and (4) "come back next week for [fill in the blank]." All other communication needs to move to other channels and methods.

What other methods and channels are there? We live in an age of so many communication options: email newsletter, text messaging, preservice set of video slides, a Facebook page. Think about creating a communications team that maps out what is said and where. You may need to retrain your church when it comes to communication, but you will be amazed at the movement you can create by simplifying and narrowing your communication from the pulpit or stage.

Now, we've been around a while. We know what a challenge that might be. Many churches have a culture built where every promotion is fair game for a stage announcement and, moreover, the sacred voice of the pastor making the announcement is a home run! Is this your experience? If so, you will need to be careful with these changes, but use ChurchOS tools to explain why you are making the changes. Use the Great Commission Engine priorities and your ONE-aware filter. Remember, connecting the ONE to us, to Jesus, and to others is your paramount concern!

Here is the beauty of the work contained in this chapter—it all goes hand in hand. If you trim back your ministry buffet, you will naturally limit what needs to be communicated. If you begin to lean into resource prioritization, you will create a defense for strategic communication. Your church will come to understand why you say what you say and how to get the information they need to get. You need to trust us. If you want to catalyze spiritual movement through a powerful weekend experience, you must be ready to capture that motion. Strategic communication must be a top priority.

So how are you doing on Resource Priority 3 (Strategic Communication)? Use our red, yellow, and green rating system and discuss your ratings as a team.

FINAL ANALYSIS

In this zero-sum environment of church leadership, where stewardship is paramount, it's pivotal to allocate and prioritize resources well. Now that you've charted your buffet, studied and rated your top resource priorities, and contemplated your squatters and cul-de-sacs . . .

Where's the action? What is emerging?

- Do you need to trim back your ministry buffet?
- Do you have nonstrategic ministries sapping resources and fostering a spirit of consumerism?
- Is relational evangelism and the power of invite your top priority?
- Have you resourced and refined your Catalytic Weekend Experience with the ONE in mind?
- Do you communicate strategically in a way that makes next steps clear and creates connection with the ONE?

Intentional Churches know how to prioritize ministry strategies, communicate effectively, and limit the ministry buffet. They voraciously fight against the consumer mentality and the development of sacred cows.

Now, in case you've skipped ahead—remember, we are still in the discovery phase. Don't take any action yet, as tempting as it might be. Keep your notes about your emerging themes and challenges. We must turn to the design phase of Intentional Growth Planning before we can move into action.

REACH ZONE, PARKS, AND PRAYERS

CROSSTOWER CHURCH—SALT LAKE CITY, UTAH

Randy Clay

"I don't know why, but I thought I needed to visit your church," Josh told me. Well, I knew why. It's because people in our church had been praying at city parks. We've been encouraging people to stop for just four or five minutes and pray for the reach zone on their way home from church.

Josh and his wife, Lindsay, came to CrossTower Church just as we started praying for those in our reach zone. They had just moved to Salt Lake City from Colorado. They had not been involved in church for a long time, but now, with a young son, they felt the tug to get back into a relationship with God. They went online to find a church to visit. They found us.

"We felt right at home the very first moment we walked in," Josh told me. "We knew we had found our church." Josh and Lindsay invited other family members to church as well. A few weeks after they all started coming, we started our initial First Steps class. All four came to the class and just soaked it in!

One Sunday, Josh told me he was ready to be baptized. Right after I baptized him, Josh baptized his nephew. That was our fastest turnaround from being baptized to baptizing someone else! Soon after, Josh's wife and sister were baptized as well.

Fast forward one year later, and Josh and Lindsay are teaching the First Steps class, excited to take this ministry to other newcomers and disciple them in the way of Jesus. Two families are now growing disciples of Jesus because we identified our reach zone, started praying for those in the reach zone, and created steps to connect them to Jesus.

FIFTY-TWO MISSION OUTPOSTS A YEAR

FAITHBRIDGE UMC—SPRING, TEXAS

Justin Teague

One can fall into the assimilation trap where you see worship at the top of the funnel as a means to an end. We can see worship only as the top of the funnel of the Engagement Pathway. It is at the top, but gathering together on the weekend has intrinsic value in and of itself. It is also discipleship.

We have fifty-two mission outpost gatherings a year. We never want to have a Sunday that is just a phone-in meeting or a gimme. We don't want to be complacent and just do our thing. We want to gather with purpose and intentionality every single week. So when we gather together, we make sure we collect an offering, count attendance, and have a teaching time, but we also have time for engaging intentional prayer. Before, there was an item on the list saying, "Let's make time to pray," but there was no measurement of the value as to what that time was. Now, it is not just a person praying over us, but we are giving people space and opportunity to pray for others and receive prayer for themselves. The music portion is more intentional as well. We are asking, "What is it we want people to walk away with? What is the big idea? Where are we leading our people for this sixty to eighty minutes? What path are we on?"

The Great Commission Engine helps with this because it's not saying worship is the most important thing or that discipleship or serving or going out on mission are the most important things. You have to do all three things to be fulfilling the Great Commission.

**For more stories and case studies, please visit
www.intentionalchurches.com.**

PHASE TWO:
DESIGN

The Intentional Growth Planning core process of ChurchOS includes four phases: discover, design, organize, and activate. You have ascended above the battlefield to discern the truth of today's battle. By rising to this altitude, you can move into phase two of the process and begin to design some key elements of your plan of attack before descending back to the thick of the fray. This vantage point will be helpful. There are three key pieces to your battle design that must be addressed: your ONE, your Engagement Pathway, and your vision.

Intentional Growth Planning™ (IGP)

Applying the ChurchOS
Living Toolbox™

1 DISCOVER   DESIGN 2

YOUR CHURCH
Great Commission Engine™
& Double Vision

ACTIVATE   ORGANIZE
4   3

SIX

WHO IS YOUR ONE?

> There is more joy in heaven over one lost sinner who repents and returns to God than over ninety-nine others who are righteous and haven't strayed away!
>
> LUKE 15:7

Mission Ventura was planted in 2011 to reach Ventura, California, and the surrounding areas with the good news of Jesus. The plant team knew this community was unique, far enough from Los Angeles to have its own identity but also very much influenced by the beach and Southern California scene. Ventura has an eclectic culture with corporate executives, Hells Angels bikers, and surfers. As Mike Hickerson, the lead pastor, described, "Ventucky is the nickname for our community here. Ventura has some grit to it and is a lot of fun. We also have an agricultural community around us as well. Our community doesn't know what it is exactly, but it knows what it is not—not Malibu, not Santa Barbara, not LA County, and not Orange County." The team adopted a wide-front-door approach, and the tag line was, and still is, Hope for Everyone.

Mission is a successful church plant by most standards. Since the outset, they have reached people and grown steadily. We started working with them a couple of years after their launch. The church leaders sensed the need to narrow their focus and install a system that allowed them to maintain steady growth and keep a handle on the complexity of their fast-growing church. They worked through the material you've been working through in this book. In doing so, they concluded they must even more narrowly focus on their ONE if they wanted to see sustained Great Commission impact.

Through diligent work to determine their ONE, they landed on the concept of Johnny Cash. Yes, Johnny Cash! In the summer of 1958, Johnny Cash moved to Ventura, and for the next decade he lived through some of his darkest days. He became involved in extramarital affairs, had some career flops, and became addicted to drugs. His early and difficult life is embodied by Ventura.

The team at Mission knows there are thousands of young men around thirty-five years old in Ventura who are suffering through the same issues Johnny did. At the center of their ministry is the ONE-aware filter. Instead of being judgmental about the ONE's behavior, they've made great efforts to understand where Johnny is coming from and actually living. This idea influences every strategy they employ. It impacts every component of their Great Commission Engine. Johnny was described by Jim Sheldon, Mission's executive pastor:

> Johnny is in his thirties. He wears a flat-billed cap and has addiction in his past (or present). He is in a committed relationship but with kids who may or may not be his. What do his kids look like? They come from a broken home, where they are shuffled back and forth each week. The family has no church background or any idea of what Sunday school is or even a classroom environment at church. The kids probably don't behave too well. Johnny and his family are just trying to keep it all together on the surface. Oh, and Johnny has a high BS meter!

The Mission team understands Johnny Cash. He is alive in their hearts, minds, actions, deeds, language, and strategies. Their connection with Johnny, combined with a heart that is white-hot to reach him and his family, is why, over the past four years, they have nearly tripled in weekend attendance, planted a church, relocated, and established community relationships like never before.

The ONE concept is a biblical idea with an upside-down consequence. By getting narrower, you become widely effective and reflective of your community. We are going to help you understand why this is important and how it works. Defining your church's ONE is a central element to ChurchOS. It is the crankshaft of the Great Commission Engine around which ministry revolves, and it's paramount to decision-making and objectifying evaluation. It is your lead filter for thought. Why? Because Jesus came to seek and save the lost. Remember Luke 15? When talking about the lost sheep, Jesus said:

Won't he leave the ninety-nine others in the wilderness and go to search for the one that is lost until he finds it? (v. 4)

And about the woman with the lost coin, Jesus said,

Won't she light a lamp and sweep the entire house and search carefully until she finds it? (v. 8)

Our loving God is committed to working tirelessly to recover the lost. We are called to the same relentless pursuit of the lost within our circle of influence. He is the Great Shepherd. He is after the ONE, and you should be as well. A focus on the ONE grows everyone.

TWO ONES TO CONSIDER

YOUR PERSONAL ONE

Each of us is called to be on mission with Christ. This means we are called to personally be active in the Great Commission. It wasn't a directive to leaders or organizations; it was and is a mission given to followers. We are to go, preach, baptize, teach, and train others to follow Jesus. It doesn't matter if you are part of a church family with this mission as its top priority, it should be yours. You are the first disciple. You are the product of the very church you lead and the gospel you teach. This means we each need our ONE for whom we are praying, seeking, and chasing. Do you have your ONE?

Furthermore, your church family should be mindful and intentional about their ONE as well. Who are each of them praying for, seeking, and chasing? Personal evangelism should be a priority for your whole church. Many books, conferences, and seminars have been developed to light the fires of personal evangelism. We are convinced this emphasis must return to our churches, and perhaps that's where your church must begin.

But this book is written to focus on an even more serious challenge. You can reach many ONEs as individuals, but is your church ready for the ONE as well? We find the latter as difficult a challenge as the first.

YOUR CHURCH'S ONE

This is a hard conversation for some leadership teams. Interestingly, it's a conversation that has some roots and history. It wasn't long ago that Willow Creek Community Church and Saddleback Community Church were teaching us to focus on "Unchurched Harry and Mary" and "Saddleback Sam," respectively. These were marketing personas that each church used to shape their ministry. This tool helped to grow both churches and impact tens of thousands, but the concept was misapplied by others and fell out of use. You had churches placing bouncers at the doors to keep out anyone who didn't match the right persona, homogenized programs that fit a narrow band of would-be followers, and a tilt toward ear-tickling, felt-need teaching meant to attract the profiled seeker but not challenge. Some churches copied Willow Creek and Saddleback wholesale, regardless of whether there was a fit with their reach zone or not. Yet with all of the past fault in application, we believe a central persona can be used to shape ministries and make decisions in a healthy way. We believe it's organic, helpful, and even biblical. We are calling for a return to ONE-awareness, and this is key to your ministry.

There is a drastic difference between contextualizing the message and strategy and watering down the gospel. The latter is about hiding the truth because we are afraid of offending someone. It may help us to get people through the door, but it's a bad way to make disciples. On the other hand, contextualizing our approach is simply making it relatable to people.

Throughout the apostle Paul's ministry, he did just that. Everywhere he went, he fully proclaimed the gospel of Christ (Rom. 15:19). The content of his message never changed, but this strategy was always adapted to his audience. Acts 16 and 17 are perfect examples of that. In Berea, Paul was able to preach to them from the Old Testament prophets (17:11). In Philippi, he met them at the river instead of at the synagogue (16:13). In Athens, he argued with the highest-ranking philosophers on their own ground, Mars Hill (17:22–31). In each case, Paul declared the same truth in a different setting with a different application. He shaped his presentation to reach his ONE.

YOUR CHURCH'S ONE: WHO?

LOCAL AND REGIONAL

The local church is a local or regional endeavor. It's meant to be *of* its surroundings. We talked about the spiritual and geographical Relational Reach Zone earlier. You must take this into account when shaping your ministry. Look at the uniqueness of some of the local church contexts in Scripture.

Rome, Corinth, and Galatia were very different places. Although Paul preached the same message of Jesus to each of them, his approach was determined by their distinct demographic. Rome, as the capital of the empire, was diverse. There was a large mixture of Jews and Gentiles by the time the church was established. So Paul spent much of his letter to the Romans talking about how salvation is for everyone.

Corinth was a metropolitan area. Although not nearly as large, it could be compared culturally and economically to New York City. With that, there were a number of unique challenges Paul had to address. Because of the class structure within the church, some ethical dilemmas were about bringing lawsuits against fellow believers (1 Cor. 6:1–11), gluttony (1 Cor. 11:17–34), and even prostitution (1 Cor. 6:12–20).

Compare that to Galatia, a rural, backwoods area. Instead of using deep philosophical arguments, he appealed to their folksy side. He referenced things like curses and personal experiences to present Christ.

In each case, the truth of the gospel remained the same, but the presentation was different because of the audience's unique setting, needs, and way of life.

A LEADERSHIP DEVICE

The ONE is simply a tool or lens through which to view and assess your church. It's an idea best held by your leaders before broad communication. Very few churches can broadly disseminate the concept of the ONE without sounding exclusive or threatening. We recommend great caution but courage at the same time. You'll find the idea very useful in time and even something your leadership can embrace easily and understand. You also want to guard against making the ONE just an idea. It's always tied to real people, real families, and real lives you are impacting.

FLUID

Because the ONE is a regional and local idea, you must address it as a team and freshen your perspective every one to three years. Why? Communities and regions change rapidly. Industries come and go, bringing new people with different viewpoints. Increased migration and immigration will mean more diverse neighborhoods.

We've worked with churches in many communities where this was true. Our work in Compton is an example. What used to be a predominantly African American community now also includes many Hispanic families and Spanish-speaking natives. East Atlanta is one of the most diverse communities in America, but it wasn't this way a generation ago.

As generations rise, their distinctiveness is displayed. This also reinforces the idea that the ONE is a tool to be used and not something to be held sacred. You are simply trying to study your community and shape your church for the broadest possible impact as your community evolves over the years.

YOUR CHURCH'S ONE

NOT MARKETING OR PANDERING

The ONE concept is not a marketing idea. This notion is actually the opposite of what we are saying. You are not trying to determine what your church is best at and then find a target market! Your church carries the same mission as the one next door and likely executes that mission similarly, but you are stewards of a unique relational network. Therefore, you are trying to discern how to shape your ministry in your neck of the woods with the best anticipation of who God is going to bring through the door.

NOT A CHOICE

In our opinion, you don't get to pick your ONE. You *discern* your ONE with the Holy Spirit's help and the trusted data of who lives in your surrounding community. In ChurchOS, we do *not* believe you should throw a dart at the board and decide who you will target. God is showing you who you should target by placing your church in a spot, at a time, for the people who need to know Jesus. Therefore, erase from your thinking the notion that you get to pick. If you want to be a multiethnic church, plant a church in a multiethnic community, follow ChurchOS principles, and you will reflect your community in time. Again, the irony of a ONE-aware focus is that you eventually reflect your community more and more because you are increasingly tapping into the relational network you were called to steward.

NOT AN OPTION

If you want to be a church that grows primarily through evangelistic reach, you must be ready for the ONE to walk through the door. We have joked there is a *Field of Dreams* principle at work in ChurchOS: "If you build it, they will come." When you start to get ready for the ONE, God starts to bring those intersections your way. We've seen it over and over again. As you develop a heart, mind, and shape for the ONE, God helps you to reach them. Great evangelistic churches have someone in mind, and they are ready to meet them before they even show up.

DISCERNING YOUR ONE

You undoubtedly know your community and those within it, your Relational Reach Zone. Some communities are diverse, and others are homogenous and similar from top to bottom. In either case, there are simple methods to narrow in on your ONE.

A BIG ASSUMPTION

If you are going to grow your kingdom impact through evangelistic effort, you must build in the assumption that your ONE is lost and not in a saving relationship with Christ. We have worked with many churches in reach zones where there was significant church experience, especially from childhood. Church experience is not the same as having a saving relationship with Christ and surrendering to his lordship. In these cases, your ONE may very well have some church experience but has yet to truly follow him.

REACH ZONE DATA

You should make an effort to understand your reach zone data within the estimated tolerable drive time of your location. In years past, you had to order demographic studies about your community, which was filled with numbers and stats that were sometimes useful but mostly not. In recent years, services have been developed to give you psychographic profiles of those in your community that are far more descriptive and less numerical or statistical. They focus on the behavioral characteristics of the community. You can easily research these services online and have a report created. This report can compare your community to the makeup of your church, adding additional insights.

MAKE A LIST

We believe you know your community and probably don't need expensive reports to understand it. Grab a whiteboard or an easel pad and, as a team, begin the journey by listing some of the people in your Relational Reach Zone.

First, who is already in your seats or pews? Think of a view from your platform. Are they doctors, lawyers, drug addicts, soldiers and sailors, teachers, mechanics, students? List those folks. They are representative of your reach zone and will be impacted by the ripple effect of your Great Commission activation.

Next, who is *not* in your seats or pews? Who do you rub shoulders with at school, the grocery store, the mall, the soccer field? Who are your members' friends? List these people as well. Most churches are reaching a cross section of their community, but undoubtedly some people are missing. One way to think of it is, what will your church look like when you become a church that reflects your community?

Finally, one of the most compelling ways to make a list of possible ONEs is to tell stories of impact. Every church has these stories, and we don't tell them often enough. One team member might say, "Think about Mike and Emma Jones. They are a great example of a family that was hurting, about to break up, and came through our doors.

We reached out, helped them through their tough time, and Emma gave her life to Jesus. Then Mike couldn't resist, and now he's plugged in and serving, along with Emma, in the kids' area. They are a great example of a couple that could make eternal, local, regional, and generational ripples because of our ministry." List your version of the Joneses and more! Tell a few stories. It will be fun and inspiring.

CHOOSE THE BULL'S-EYE

Once your list is made, you must decide as a team who you are going to narrowly consider when designing your church. This might be tough, but it is so important. Deep breath. Like we said earlier, you can't be all things to all people, so who do you have in mind when you are shaping your ministry going forward?

Here are some thoughts we've found that can help you in this decision:

- You aren't going to reject people who aren't your ONE.
- By preparing for your ONE, you are honoring God's local call on your ministry. Your community will change and so should your ONE.
- Through relational evangelism, you are going to reach many people in your Relational Reach Zone who are connected to your ONE.
- The lives connected to your ONE might or might not look like or be similar to your ONE. This doesn't change the need for focus.
- In time, you will reflect your community. This is what God wants for your church!

Getting close? We hope so. Once you've nailed it, let's dig in just a little further by answering the following questions:

- Who is our ONE?
- How old is our ONE?

- What is our ONE's marital status?
- Does our ONE have kids? How many?
- What are a couple characteristics of our ONE?

GET TO KNOW YOUR ONE

DEFINE YOUR ONE'S CORE MOTIVATORS

If you really want to begin the translation of your ONE to your ministry, you must nail down your ONE's core motivators. Remember, your ONE does not follow Jesus, and what motivates this ONE today at a deep level will change as they come to know and follow Christ. We must know them in order to connect with them.

You can diagnose your ONE's core motivators by looking at where they spend their time, energy, money, and attention. These are the four commodities of life. We all have them and use them in unique ways. You can also look into the domains of their life for discernment: family, children, work, career, relationships, entertainment, material goods, etc. Here is a simple process to help you get there. Discuss and take notes as a team.

Ask these simple evidentiary questions. We've also given you some sample answers. Where does your ONE spend his/her:

- Kid time, energy, money, attention? (soccer, travel ball, lessons)
- Relationship time, energy, money, attention? (self-help book, nights out with friends)
- Work time, energy, money, attention? (stays late, works weekends, getting GED)
- Entertainment or material time, energy, money, attention? (hunting trips, season tickets, fancy car)

Now dig in. What lies beneath these actions? Take a minute. You almost always start with surface answers. This is deep stuff. Think of the ONE's motivating forces. Here are some answers from our work with churches across the nation:

- Loneliness
- Distrust of authority
- Debt and financial instability
- Better life for kids
- Excellent, curated experiences
- Escape or addiction
- Keeping up with friends or status
- Relational brokenness and ill equipped

Finally, narrow in as a team on your ONE's top four motivators. Yes, top four! We have found that less is more in ChurchOS. Just focus on the big four in the coming season and how those can impact your ministry. You are beginning to build your ONE-aware filter.

NAME YOUR ONE

We encourage you to name your ONE and make the idea really come alive. Mission Ventura named theirs Johnny Cash because the name made sense to their community. A church in Cincinnati named theirs Jack Cooper because the name personified the former Catholic school–educated guy in that region. Jack has lots of friends and doesn't need more community. He wants to understand the religion he has grown up with his whole life. A church in Southern California chose the name Angelica because the Hispanic, single working mother was their chosen ONE. They have shaped their ministry in preparation for her, her family, and her friends. So name him or her. Use the name often. Make it common language for you and your leadership team.

DEVELOP A PERSONA AND A DESCRIPTION

The final step in getting to know your ONE so you can build a filter for decision-making is to write out a persona or profile of their life. Early in this chapter we gave you an idea of how Mission Ventura made their description of Johnny Cash come alive. Nearly every team member can repeat that descriptive language. A midwestern church came up with the following description for their ONE:

Joe is a twenty-five-year-old family man with two kids and a significant other, though the kids may not all be his. He wants what's best for his family, but he often struggles with parenting and the basics of trying to provide for all of them. He works hard and for many hours a week but usually is just getting by financially. The significant other works outside of the home but not full time because babysitting is too expensive.

Joe has had a rough past. In high school and his early twenties he spent time exploring alcohol, girls, and drugs, leaving him with baggage, such as an addiction to pornography and other things to cope with stress. He is insecure in himself but often tries to act like he's got it all together. The inside Joe is different from the outside Joe, and this hurts his ability to have authentic relationships with other males. He doesn't want anyone to get too close to him and know what he is really going through. It takes a long time for his barriers to get broken down.

He wants to make a difference in this world to make up for the inadequacy he feels within himself. He feels good helping others and often goes unnoticed. Joe would agree to projects if someone asked, but a general announcement is not going to work very often. People who Joe looks up to are churchgoers, and that is how he got invited. He is starting to realize he needs to step up his responsibility and become a better parent and husband/spouse.

NOW WHAT?

REEVALUATE YOUR GREAT COMMISSION ENGINE

This is a good time to review chapter 4. Now that you have a lens for decision-making and evaluation, you can more readily and capably put the ONE-aware filter on all that you do. In chapter 4 we objectified at the highest level what must be true in each of the component parts of the Great Commission Engine, but we also told you to use your ONE-aware filter without it being fully developed.

For example, Sy Huffer, pastor of College Heights Christian Church in Joplin, Missouri, did this with his team at a leadership retreat.

> As part of the retreat, we had each person on the team arrive at the facility and pick up a description of the ONE, and then drive away from the facility. We asked them to drive back as if they were coming to church for the first time as our ONE: Jessica, an unmarried thirty-year-old mom working in the medical community and finishing school. What is she thinking as she pulls into the parking lot? Can she tell where to drop off her kids? Is she going to the right door? Is there clear direction and signage? How does she locate the worship center? What is she confused or anxious about? Does our language make sense to her?

The team debriefed using Four Helpful Lists (of which you should have a growing familiarity!) and prioritized some immediate actions they could take. The team immediately went to work. You could do the same for each of the Great Commission Engine components.

When the team at Mission Ventura took a hard look at their ministry in light of Johnny Cash, a lot was adjusted (and continues to be on the table for evaluation). Here are a few action items they pushed through:

- The team read *The Big Book of Alcoholics Anonymous*[1] to better understand their ONE
- Began a recovery ministry led by a recovering ONE
- Trained volunteers in kids' areas because the ONE's children will likely be acting up and unfamiliar with church environments

- Changed the lobby experience and added Pearl Jam to the lobby playlist
- Added ONEs to the usher and greeter teams, plus training
- Developed men's outreach events and first steps for men's groups
- Proactively began ministry to homeless people alongside community partners and invited ONEs to serve and volunteer
- Changed the first-step plan to connect with the ONE's felt needs

You get the picture. What can you adjust in your Great Commission Engine? Debrief using Four Helpful Lists, prioritize, and take some action.

USE IT!

You must make it a point to not only refresh your ONE persona and decision-making filter, you must use it!

Renaissance Church in Summit, New Jersey, was planted in 2001 to impact the affluent communities of Short Hills, Millburn, Chatham, and Summit. It was the vision of a Christ-following investment banker at Goldman Sachs who had grown up in the area and met Christ while away at college.

Renaissance is a poignant example of the power of the ONE. When it was founded, there was a one-page, easy-to-read description of their ONE. It was a representation of the founder's life before he knew Christ. If a church was going to be effective at reaching people like him, it must take this into account and be ready to meet him where he is living pre-Jesus.

Here are some highlights from the description of Richard, the ONE identified by Renaissance:

- **GENERAL:** Richard and his wife's affluence is consistent with the community in which they live. Each is likely a product of an Ivy League (or similar) education. Their success surpasses their age.

- **CAREER:** Richard is highly successful within his field, such as the financial arena. He works long hours and most likely commutes via train. His wife may or may not have a career but stays equally busy.
- **FAMILY:** Kids are of central value. Education and other activities are very important and ultracompetitive. It matters where they go to school.
- **FINANCES:** They have achieved a noteworthy level of wealth for their age, but time is the most important commodity.
- **RELATIONSHIPS:** He portrays strength and independence, but this is a facade. This also inhibits the development of real relationships.
- **FAITH:** Richard and his wife have had religious experiences but not relationships with God. He and his wife find themselves having questions of faith, but the church they've experienced is not a place to get real answers.

When we began working with Renaissance, it was clear they were a team that knew and understood their community and their ONE. They were very effective at many things, but they had one weak spot. Richard and his family were coming to church, meeting Jesus, and beginning to grow. But the church was struggling at in-depth discipleship. They had started a Wednesday-night Bible study, but attendance was low at best.

The answer hit us like a ton of bricks. If Richard is going to grow up in Christ, if he is going to study and be mentored by other Christ followers, it's likely going to have to happen on a train! Richard leaves the house at 6:00 a.m., gets on the train to Manhattan, comes home by 8:00 p.m., and works some on most Saturdays. The plan to disciple Richard cannot involve a Wednesday-night Bible study. The plan was to develop a system to mentor Richard on the train.

This is a lesson we will never forget. You must keep the ONE-aware filter in front of you and use it over and over and over!

TRUST IT!

You will only know you got it right by using it. You can always adjust. We've seen it work again and again, and it's the centerpiece of ChurchOS.

One of our favorite stories of the power of the ONE is Mount Olive General Baptist Church in Winslow, Indiana. The team from Mount Olive attended one of our regional events where we discussed the basics of ChurchOS, and they strongly embraced the idea of the ONE. They immediately put it into practice.

Over the next few months, Mount Olive saw dramatic Great Commission activation. On one Sunday, they baptized twenty-two people! In an interview at the denomination's annual gathering, the senior pastor explained that pinpointing their ONE was the single biggest catalyst of their growing impact. They redesigned every element of the site-to-seat-to-street experience for the ONE. They also adjusted prayer, care, and other ministries—all for their ONE. Today they are averaging more than a hundred in weekend attendance, with seventy people proceeding through the commitment to become members. Their amazing courage is leading to more than double kingdom impact. It works!

Do you remember what we said about the *Field of Dreams* effect? It's clear that when we join the heart of Jesus for the lost and begin to discern, with the Holy Spirit's help, what that *really* means to our church, *and* you make courageous adjustments, he meets us in that effort. He brings holy intersections with ONEs who need to know him and our churches. All for his glory.

Intentional Churches understand the two-sided coin of personal evangelism—the ONE of each Ninety-Niner and a church that is ready to reach the ONE. They know how to keep the fires of evangelism burning white hot.

The first design element in ChurchOS is the ONE. Understanding the identity of the ONE is central to the system and must be constantly monitored. Next, we're going to look at your Engagement Pathway, the primary system for connecting the ONE to you, Jesus, and one another.

DESIGNING FOR JOHNNY

MISSION CHURCH—VENTURA, CALIFORNIA

Mike Hickerson and Jim Sheldon

As a church of 600 with a goal to be 1,200, we knew we would have to move. The subleased 16-screen theater could not be our permanent home. So we ended up designing a space. The ethos of mission that attracts a Johnny Cash–type was definitely a part of the design process.

We had conversations around Johnny Cash with our facility architect and designers. One of the things we did was to pick a room that was important to Johnny Cash. We picked the living room. We also realized we had to look local and handcrafted. Everything needed to be excellent without being too polished. We don't want to use anything that looks mass produced. We even hand-drew a whimsical map of Ventura—creating a mural that is 30 feet high. People walk in and they know this is our place.

We sacrificed usable space in our building to create a lobby that was inviting and welcoming. It communicates, "Hey, come and hang out. You are invited to stay." Hospitality is a big deal for us, so we have a 5,000-square-foot lobby in a 32,000-square-foot building. We didn't want to communicate that the lobby was just a place to pass through. We wanted it to be a place where people could hang out and talk.

We also don't have a greenroom. It is a little bit of our ethos here. We don't have to hide or need to get away. There is no removal of the pastors and the people. "Hope for Everyone" is on a huge sign above our auditorium. From the beginning, we have had a simplified brand. Even our initial logo was black and white and simple. Without feeling cold, it is clean.

Within two weeks of moving into the new building, we were asking what it would look like if we doubled again, because we were already running more than 1,200. We are unrelenting in that desire to grow. It's not that we just want numbers. We want to stay focused on the ONE and eternal impact and not the gravitational pull inward. Thinking in terms of double impact breaks your thinking. If you have to think about double impact, then what you are doing now does not work. You are thinking about effectiveness rather than efficiency.

IT'S TIME TO EXCEL

FIRST CHURCH—BURLINGTON, KENTUCKY

Tommy Baker

One of my mentors told me early in my youth ministry days to excel at bringing kids to Christ. And it's true of all leaders in the church. We can never take our eyes off the people who are not yet within the church. To do that, we must be principle driven and strategic. Why? There isn't enough time to do what we like. Be willing to make the tough decisions, and be willing to say no. We must increase our burden for those who do not know Christ. It isn't just about how many people attend on the weekend. We want lives to be changed. There has to be transformation taking place.

**For more stories and case studies, please visit
www.intentionalchurches.com.**

SEVEN

THE ENGAGEMENT PATHWAY

So let's not get tired of doing what is good. At just the right time we will reap a harvest of blessing if we don't give up.

GALATIANS 6:9

Imagine you are the captain of a ship racing to the rescue of a sinking ship, much like the *Carpathia* steaming at full speed to the last known location of the *Titanic*. What does that feel like? Surreal? The scene is idyllic. The ocean seems calm. The clear sky is full of stars. But the work at hand could not be more urgent. There are highs and lows as you find masses of lifeless bodies floating on the ocean's surface. Your crew is plucking the living out of the water, one by one, and they're filling the deck quickly. You breathe new life into them and assure them they're okay now. They're safe now. The rescuers, however, can't move fast enough, but you know they must be careful and orderly at the same time. Conflicted and under pressure, you do the best you can.

Church leadership is a lot like that. We know for a fact you've experienced the highs and lows in ministry. We know you have been conflicted and under pressure, doing the best you can. Perhaps your town feels calm at the moment, but the work at hand has never been more urgent or meaningful. We wish every church had a similar sense of urgency with a careful, orderly plan to save as many as possible.

And this is why we are about to lay out the details of a pivotal design element of ChurchOS. The Engagement Pathway is meant to help you pluck as many people as possible from the abyss. It will also help you breathe new life into them and assure them all is well. They are loved and have a purpose. It will even help to give them a job on the very same rescue ship! So let's get started.

A HOLY SENSE OF URGENCY

We want you to imagine the life of your ONE as they intersect with your church. If you've been following along, you now have a name for your ONE and a list of characteristics of the ONE's life. You know if she has a family or where she works. You know if he is married or if he's a single parent. You are coming to understand the essence of your ONE's life.

Now, it's time for the ONE to walk through the front door of your church. You've been praying for this moment. You've been leading the Ninety-Nine, and they are investing and inviting their ONEs. Preferably, the ONE walked through the door on the arm of a friend who is connected to your church already. But perhaps they didn't. The ONE and her family have been circling the parking lot, deciding if it's worth the effort to park and go through the door. They are hurting and in need. Finally, they get up the courage and begin the trek, not knowing what to expect. It's the moment of truth. What happens next could make an eternal difference.

Your ability to double your kingdom impact is directly connected to your ability to engage and connect with your ONE. We've said it before but it bears repeating: If you do not connect your ONE with you, Jesus, and others, you lose. You cannot go on an eternal difference-making journey with them if you have not effectively connected to them. You want your first steps of connection to be simple and intuitive, so the ONE can't help but walk through them. Even more powerfully, your Ninety-Nine walk with your ONE through them as well!

The Engagement Pathway is one of the universal top-level strategies that must be developed by every church. It's one of the five key components in the Great Commission Engine because it is universal. (Refer back to chapter 3 for a reminder.) We talked about it briefly earlier in the book, but now we are going to take a deeper look at how to build an effective but custom pathway for connections. We are also going to show you how and why measuring it is vital, because you can actually measure the Engagement Pathway and know if you are on track to double your kingdom impact. It's just that important.

THE FUNNEL OF ENGAGEMENT

The visual we use to explain the Engagement Pathway is a funnel. Why? It's simple. The Engagement Pathway is all about getting people to move—toward you, toward Jesus, and toward others. We move them through the door to take a baby step of engagement into a group, onto a service team, and back out into the reach zone to impact their world. Each step is deliberately connected to the next. It's about

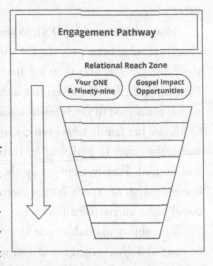

getting people to move into the activities that help them grow. Into the progressive commitments that put them on mission with Jesus and your church!

Memorize the next sentence. *The Engagement Pathway is not a discipleship pathway.* Maybe you read the title of this chapter and said, "Oh, we already have a discipleship pathway." But they're not the same thing. The Engagement Pathway connects the ONE to you, Jesus, and others. It also connects the ONE to the core functions of your Great Commission Engine. In these environments and through the ministry that is done there, they will become committed disciples over time. God will meet them there and grow them. *You* don't grow the church or the people in the church. *God* does. You may have a well-oiled discipleship process that is bearing fruit, but we believe, when it comes to the ONE, the Engagement Pathway is of first importance. What you do with Pistons 1 (Catalytic Weekend Experience), 2 (Life-Changing Relationships), and 3 (Surrendered Living) is pivotal, but it doesn't matter if the ONE isn't connected to you.

THE HEADWATERS OF ENGAGEMENT

At the beginning, you need to understand what the top of the funnel represents. There are two primary areas that feed into the Engagement Pathway. These should all be familiar to you if you've been following along. First, there is your Relational Reach Zone. The most natural source for engagement is the connection of your ONE to your Ninety-Nine within a particular driving radius around your church. There is also a plethora of gospel impact opportunities in your reach zone (far more numerous than you realize). A well-envisioned and trained church family has gospel impact opportunities at every turn.

With tremendous potential surrounding your church, the key question is how your church will tap into these gospel impact opportunities, especially as they relate to the relationships of your Ninety-Nine. There are three things at work that must be true for this potential to be tapped.

A WELL-EQUIPPED ARMY

We believe your best tap into the reach zone is a well-equipped Ninety-Nine, ready to help you win your Jerusalem and Antioch to Christ. We talked about this briefly in chapter 6. You cannot activate the Great Commission without an army of Ninety-Niners ready to go to battle with you. They must be envisioned, trained, and equipped to reach their ONE. They know who their ONEs are and pray for them regularly. They are ready for spiritual conversations and know the strategy of your church to reach the ONE.

THE POWER OF INVITATION

Your church must develop a culture of invitation. There are two types of invitation to consider. Invitation into a relationship usually comes first. Whether it was the Lord sitting next to a well on a hot day and having a conversation (John 4:6–7) or Paul talking with people in the Athenian market (Acts 17:17), normal and natural relationships produce connection. Next, the power of invite extends to your church. Your Ninety-Nine must shamelessly be prepared to invite their ONE into a relationship with your church. That can happen many ways in a church running ChurchOS. It can be an outreach event, a small group, a special event, and more. And, yes, it certainly can be a Piston 1 Catalytic Weekend Experience. In fact, that's often where it starts.

A ONE-AWARE ENGAGEMENT PATHWAY

Your church must be prepared for this invitation into relationship and be prepared to produce a meaningful connection. Building the best pathway you have is the primary method to take full advantage of the power of invitation. If built well, you can anticipate connection. Your Engagement Pathway must be clear, well communicated, and constantly tended. It must be measured. Simple. Slippery. Yes, slippery! Meaning it's built so intuitively for the ONE that she and her family can't help but take the next step toward you. You've lowered the barriers to entry so low that the ONE finds it easy to connect to you, Jesus, and others.

Do you see how it's all coming together? Attention to each component of the Great Commission Engine matters. Now that you know your ONE, you can be more honest about the status of these key elements. You need to be a spiritual movement hawk because the Engagement Pathway is all about movement. Now you are ready to put it all together to drive double kingdom impact by connecting hundreds or thousands of ONEs to you, Jesus, and others.

We think the best way to help you with designing your Engagement Pathway is to walk you through the principles that make a pathway work and then show you an example.

THE SIX PRINCIPLES OF THE ENGAGEMENT PATHWAY

We've found there are six principles that make a great Engagement Pathway work. At some level, your church may already have some of these principles in play. But we must caution you: Give all six a careful read without skipping over any because something seems familiar. Go into this with an open sense of discovery and remain open to some new ideas or refreshing what may be currently stale. After you learn what these principles are, review the example to see where the principles pop up and embed themselves between the lines.

PRINCIPLE 1: OPT-IN

The key to a good Engagement Pathway is that it's built with opt-in thinking. You want it to be so simple and intuitive that the ONE can't help but opt into it. Once they have opted in or taken their first step, you can increase your engagement and response to their first step.

Building simple opt-in steps for the ONE is both art and science. It takes experimentation and the discipline of constant improvement (the kaizen principle). Here is an example of the sequence of changes and improvements from a church that worked on their Engagement Pathway over several years:

- Change #1: Build a room for guests, and staff it with nice people to answer questions and promote it every week.
- Change #2: Move the room from the second floor to a spot near the lobby. (The ONE doesn't want to walk upstairs after the service; they want to get to the car.)
- Change #3: Attach the room to the sanctuary to make it simple to enter after the service.
- Change #4: Train the staff in the guests' room to act like concierges, tour guides, and pastoral experts rather than information desk attendants.
- Change #5: Put an exit door from the room so the ONE doesn't feel intimidated about entering.
- Change #6: Change the decor to match the tastes of the ONE. Become more relevant in appearance.
- Change #7: Offer a gift, such as a Starbucks card, and more for anyone who stops by.
- Change #8: Promote the guests' room every week for anyone who has a question, would like to meet with someone, or wants to take a next step of some kind.

Through each adjustment, this church improved the effectiveness of its guest connection room by ten times over a few years. But note, the list above represents a decade of constant assessment and improvements! Set your expectations realistically. This church set big goals for the early steps of connection, and it caused the team to constantly keep the Engagement Pathway in front of them. It's amazing how goals for your Engagement Pathway can lead to growth.

PRINCIPLE 2: SIMPLE STEPS (NOT GIANT LEAPS)

Simple-step thinking and design is a way of life. It can be applied everywhere. We have talked about it earlier, but we want to drive the idea a little deeper. You must constantly work to break down the steps of increasing commitment into small, easy steps the ONE can and will take. We often say you have to work from the ONE back to you, meaning what can and will they do right now in order to get them to the place you want them to be later.

Churches are notorious for building barriers to entry rather than simple, doable steps. They build giant leaps, not intuitive, incremental movements for the ONE. Here are a couple of examples of giant leaps versus simple steps.

- *Giant-Leap Design:*
  - Fill out this information card and give us all of your details.
  - Sign up to serve in the nursery (for life or at least indefinitely).
  - Go to the lobby and look through the pamphlets on the wall. Pick out a small group you'd like to attend.
  - Begin tithing tomorrow (when we know you've never before regularly given anything to anyone).
  - Come back this afternoon for our four-hour membership class and potluck dinner (despite your favorite team's game starting at 1:00 P.M.).
- *Simple-Step Design:*
  - Give me only the information I need. I'll make sure someone follows up with you.
  - Let's find your gifts and passions and try out a serving spot for a couple of weeks.
  - Let me help you find the right small group. What's your age? Where do you live? Do you have kids?
  - Can you start to give regularly? How about a regular weekly commitment while you pray about how to grow over time in your giving?
  - Attend our membership class, which happens at the same time as the services. We'll keep your kids so you can attend this important next step in your journey.

Do you get the picture? Simple steps must become your way of life, especially concerning the ONE. If your Engagement Pathway isn't working well, and people aren't taking the steps you hoped they would, take it upon yourself to figure out why. It's likely a breakdown in your simple-step engineering.

PRINCIPLE 3: RELATIONAL

A great Engagement Pathway gets a person involved and a relationship established as soon as possible. Remember the seven relationships rule we mentioned earlier in the book from Gary McIntosh and Charles Arn (once a person has made seven friendship connections at your church, they consider themselves a part of your church family). The sooner the ONE knows and feels known, the sooner the ONE will feel connected to your church and will call your church home.

Here are some practical ideas on how to make the Engagement Pathway relational early in the connection process:

- Staff your next steps or connections areas with knowledgeable and trained people. The gift mix of this personnel matters.
- If you have a membership or first-step class or workshop, be sure to make it interactive and use table conversation. Have the hosts get to know the people at the table and follow up with them.
- In general, take an ushering mentality to the next level: usher people to the next step they need to take. If they are signing up for the kids camp, escort them to the sign-up area or help them sign up. If they're having difficulty finding their car in the parking lot, help them!
- Place the same greeters and ushers in similar spots every week so they can spot the new faces. Train them on what to say and how to manage these critical early interactions with the ONE.

PRINCIPLE 4: SEQUENTIAL

People think and move in steps and sequences. It's natural if you have taken step one to look for step two. Remember that people do not want to feel processed; they just want the next step to make sense.

Map out the typical sequence of connection for your ONE. This is the beginning of a good Engagement Pathway design. What will the ONE want to do first? What would they like to do next? And so on. Again, think and design simple steps, but design them sequentially and logically. For instance, if you teach the value of life-changing relationships, immediately offer opportunities to join a small group. The same is true for teaching about spiritual gifts and then offering opportunities to serve.

PRINCIPLE 5: MEANINGFUL

The Engagement Pathway must be built to deliver and add value for the ONE. Where are they actually living? What are the driving forces in the ONE's life and family? What do they really need? As you design your Engagement Pathway, rework your description of the ONE and look at the motivators in his life. Refresh your memory and use it as an overlay. Remember to always use your One-aware filter.

We have seen churches miss it on this front while other churches knock it out of the park. One church had a small group commitment inserted into its Engagement Pathway, but in this case, the ONE wanted nothing to do with more friends. He had friends up to his eyeballs! What he needed was a better understanding of the ancient religion around which he had grown up but didn't now understand. The church started simple Bible classes on Wednesday nights, and engagement went through the roof.

PRINCIPLE 6: MEASURABLE

You can measure your Engagement Pathway and know if you are on pace to double your kingdom impact or not. The connection and transformation of the ONE into a fully committed Ninety-Nine on mission with you and Christ is the leading marker of where you are headed in both the short and long terms. You can tell if your five-year vision is on pace or not. But you must first design and set your own measurables and goals. Each pathway is unique, as is each road to double kingdom impact.

Here's an example of a church that has done just that. Don't copy it. Learn from it and look for these principles at work in your church. Then get to work on one of your own!

EXAMPLE: FIRST CHURCH ENGAGEMENT PATHWAY (WITH MEASURABLE GOALS)

This example pathway is real and in use by several churches we know. For the sake of the example, we will call this the First Church Engagement Pathway. It is the expected pathway of connection for the ONE while knowing that people will connect in all kinds of ways. Regardless, it is the primary defined, measured, and controlled engagement system for First Church.

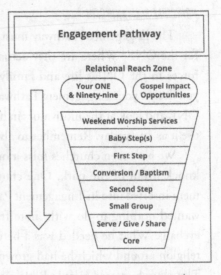

WEEKEND WORSHIP SERVICES

At the top of the Engagement Pathway is the weekend worship service. If you are building a primary dedicated system, what is the likely point of first connection? First Church believes it is the weekend services (Piston 1: Catalytic Weekend Experience). The same is likely true for your church. In fact, after hundreds of Engagement Pathways have been built with our help, we've yet to see one that didn't anticipate the ONE's connection would likely begin there. Here's what First Church knows, so take note.

This first step of connection will probably occur at the invitation of one of your Ninety-Nine. Remember the principles of Piston 1 (Catalytic Weekend Experience) from chapter 3. When they encounter you, your church, and your Ninety-Nine, you must be ready for the ONE's total experience. It is a site-to-seat-to-street total experience, and if one link in the experience is weak, you may lose the potential of connecting with the ONE.

Through incredible worship and life-changing preaching, the ONE will inevitably be impacted by the power of the Holy Spirit. The Spirit draws people to Christ. The Spirit convicts. The Spirit prompts and the ONE will eventually be prompted to act—the first actions the ONE takes may be visible or not. But one day the ONE will take the first step of true connection toward your church.

After each component of the Engagement Pathway in this example, we are going to discuss the measurables. Measuring the effectiveness of your Engagement Pathway should be a top priority. The following are measurables and goals for First Church's Engagement Pathway.

First Church Weekend Worship Services Measurables and Goals

First Church uses attendance at the weekend worship services as the baseline against which to measure their Engagement Pathway. It is the primary measurable. We spoke earlier in the book about average weekend attendance (AWA) and how you must determine a counting methodology for Piston 1 (Catalytic Weekend Experience). The simple approach for First Church is to count every adult, child, and student as best as possible. The goal for this first step in the Engagement Pathway is to grow by 15 percent or more each year (to double the kingdom impact of this component in five years or less).

BABY STEPS

First Church knows it must provide a simple step of connection from the weekend worship services when the ONE is ready to take action. They call this a baby step and have worked on multiple steps of connection over the years. They have engineered this step to be just right for the ONE, but the job of adjusting and improving the effectiveness of this first encounter is never complete. Again, if you believe people engage in steps rather than programs, then the first steps they take are the most important.

At First Church, they knew their ONE was likely intimidated at the idea of connection, so the barrier to taking that step must be low. They experimented with various rooms throughout the building, attached to the sanctuary, and so on. Now they are using a carpeted area in the lobby with a sign on the wall: First Steps at First Church? The carpeted area is crewed by friendly people who know their first order of business is to serve the ONE who steps onto the carpet and to see if they are interested in attending a class called First Step (which we will cover next). First Church also has developed a prayer-and-care area after each service, because they sense there is hurt and desperation in the life of their ONE. First Church holds a public invitation for prayer and salvation every week, but they realize the ONE is likely too intimidated to take such a step, and they saw a more private option was necessary.

Finally, First Church knows a connection card is not the best method to invite the ONE to take the early steps of connection. People today simply do not want to share too much information before they know and trust you. Still, the church uses a connection card, but it is an alternate, not the primary, means of connecting. Instead, First Church tries to inject relationship as soon as possible into their Engagement Pathway, and thus they staff their baby steps with well-equipped, trained, and personable volunteers.

First Church Baby Steps Measurables and Goals

First Church measures and sets goals for their Engagement Pathway in relation to their weekend worship services. This makes sense to them because they built the pathway to move people from outside the church into a deep life in the church, knowing the journey likely starts with the weekend worship services. So they measure success as throughput in relation to what is happening in the worship services (the top of the funnel).

The baby-step goal for First Church is 100 percent of AWA through a baby step in a given year. For instance, if AWA is averaging

1,000, they expect 1,000 baby steps to be taken in that year. This huge goal sets tremendous expectation on a couple of things. First, it recognizes you can expect your AWA represents about 3,000 (AWA x 3), the number of people who already connect to your church and call it home. If each of them joins the mission, the potential for reach greatly increases. (We covered the math that matters in chapter 5.) There is far more opportunity for connections than you expect. Also, if they are building a primary pathway, and you have the ONE in mind, early steps matter. So they focus most of their energy at the top of the funnel. The journey starts there.

FIRST STEP CLASS

First Church offers a series of one-hour classes called First Step as an orientation to both the church and the Christian life. They know their ONE well and have designed their primary Engagement Pathway with them in mind. This includes the First Step class. Over the years, First Church has done many things to adjust and improve their First Step class experience. They continually design and redesign it to make sense for the early faith journey of their ONE. It would be so easy to design it in a way that misses where the ONE really lives—and they've made that mistake before. They know if you do not connect with the ONE where they are actually living, they will not go on a spiritual journey with you and they may not meet Christ.

This is a good point to mention that what is contained in these simple paragraphs represents years of work! We are giving you a living example to cast a vision for a well-run Engagement Pathway. In our experience, it is rarely built quickly, and it must be constantly refined.

Over the years, First Step class has been worked and reworked. Today, it is offered on Sunday mornings (concurrent with worship services), and the ONE is encouraged to attend. First Church has multiple worship services, so the ONE can opt to go to First Step when they would normally attend church, or they can attend a service and then go to First Step during another service.

Here are some additional tweaks to the First Step class that occurred over the years. First Church only promotes the first week of the four-week series of classes. They feel the likelihood of the ONE committing to four weeks is far less than committing to just one. The other three weeks of the First Step class are promoted at the end of the first week. Week one of First Step is conducted in a party atmosphere, and the event is catered with incredible food. The ONE is made to feel very special. They are given a gift and told that a gift will be given each week if they come back. The first gift is an easy-to-read Bible, because 60 percent of the ONEs attending don't own a Bible—or one they can read. (Talk about knowing your ONE!)

What is covered over the four weeks of the First Step class? It is built for the ONE of First Church. In their transient environment, here is what First Church believes their ONE needs to know if they make it to the First Step class.

- Week 1: Who is Jesus? (Invitation to accept Christ is offered.)
- Week 2: What is the Bible and how do I read it?
- Week 3: What is prayer and how do I pray?
- Week 4: How do I have a daily relationship with Jesus?

One more thing: if you combine First Church's First Step class and its Second Step class, you get what closely resembles a traditional membership class. Remember, this is an example of how one church built their Engagement Pathway, but there is a lot to learn. We will take a minute when we discuss Second Step to apply this to your church.

First Church First Step Class Measurables and Goals

The measurables for First Step are attendance, completion, and salvations. Again, First Church sets a high bar for themselves, expecting their Baby Steps to deliver the ONE to the First Step class. The goal for attendance is 20 percent of their AWA in one year, meaning 200 in total attendance if First Church is averaging 1,000 in AWA. The completion goal is 100 percent. Through incredible effort and constant improvement, they are averaging nearly 98 percent completion of all four weeks. Salvations was a learned goal. They thought a small portion of decisions for Christ would come from the First Step class, but they immediately realized people needed to clearly understand the gospel, had questions about baptism, and would respond once these concerns were addressed. Since then, the goal for salvations is a minimum of 35 percent per session.

CONVERSION/BAPTISM

First Church decided to put conversion and baptism in their pathway to create internal accountability for this step in the life of the ONE. The tradition of the church is to offer a gospel invitation often and follow decisions for Christ with water baptism. This created an expectation that it would be a part of the Engagement Pathway's engineering attention. First Church wants to move the ONE toward them, Jesus, and others. We mentioned in the last section that First Church realized the Engagement Pathway is actually delivering 32 to 50 percent of their conversions because of the questions and concerns of the ONE, which created barriers to the moment of decision. That is not the only opportunity for conversion and baptism, however.

First Church has special baptism days, gives a gospel invitation at every service, and clearly explains this at the First Steps class. The constant attention to moving the ONE, as well as multiple methods of promotion, has led to great success in this evangelistically minded church. Conversions and baptisms are a routine part of its Piston 1 (Catalytic Weekend Experience).

First Church Conversion/Baptism Measurables and Goals

The measurables for conversion and baptism at First Church are the total number of baptisms in a given year as a percentage of AWA. Their goal is to baptize 20 percent of their AWA. If they are averaging 1,000 in AWA, they expect to baptize 200 people that year. This again is a high bar, and setting this goal places an appropriate pressure on the team to make sure the top of the Engagement Pathway delivers a high number of people to the First Step class. It also forces them to engage in other creative strategies on a routine basis, including baptism emphasis, personal evangelism training, creative invite events, and more.

SECOND STEP CLASS

First Church is committed to breaking the spiritual journey into bite-size steps for their ONE. As a reminder, the First Step class walks them through the fundamentals of how to have a personal faith and relationship with Jesus. This is because they've learned the ONE needs to hear this clearly, and it's urgent because their ONE sometimes leaves town quickly. Second Step is the next level of what the ONE needs to know to fully engage First Church's and Jesus' mission. It's built to create owners of this mission, and it's offered directly on the heels of the First Step class.

If you jump to the end of the First Church Engagement Pathway, you will notice the word *Core*. It is the dream of First Church to create true owners of the ministry and mission of Christ, that is, people who live out Christ's mission every day, everywhere. They've built their Engagement Pathway with this in mind, but all the while they are connecting and developing their ONE! This means they must carefully, courageously, and quickly build simple steps for the ONE to take toward this end. They believe if they do this, they will create an army of future Ninety-Niners who will help them win their city and region to Christ. They will have a core that will ignite invitations in their reach zone.

The Second Step class is offered on Sunday morning at the same time as the First Step class. First Step runs back-to-back for four weeks, and Second Step is offered on four back-to-back weeks, making a total of eight weeks for the two classes. Since the pattern was created through First Step, commitment to the Second Step class is strong. Second Step is promoted as an opportunity to be on mission with First Church and Jesus, becoming true owners of the ministry.

So what is an owner at First Church? To promote ownership, First Church defined it in terms of five commitments (we will speak later about the difference between ownership and membership):

- SALVATION: Accept Christ as your Lord and Savior.
- GROUP: Participate regularly in a dedicated small group.
- SERVE: Find a place of regular, gifted service.
- GIVE: Give regularly and grow in your giving as God leads. (First Church teaches about tithing and sacrificial giving but only requires a regular weekly commitment to be an owner. The ONE must be on the generosity journey.)
- SHARE: Share your faith regularly, and live a life of invitation.

First Church is taking newly minted Christians (who are probably still a bit of a mess) and giving them a simple-step pathway to join the greatest mission on earth! They trust God to develop the ONE in time, and they see their role as assisting the ONE. If the ONE will make those commitments, and First Church facilitates what it takes, the ONE's life will never be the same. And neither will First Church's!

Second Step is four weeks long and covers the topics of giving, serving, small groups, and sharing your faith, all with a minimum requirement of commitment for owners. There is an opportunity to become an owner if the participants commit to each requirement. First Church offers the eight-week series of First Step and Second Step four times each year: early in the year, after Easter, summer, and mid-autumn. So far, through simple-step design and constant improvement, they have seen nearly 80 percent of those who begin the journey of First Step complete all eight weeks. To drive that percentage higher, First Church is currently working on makeup material for those who miss a week.

First Church Second Step Class Measurables and Goals
The measurables for Second Step are attendance, completion, group placements, serving placement, and new giving units. Again, First

Church sets a high bar by expecting their baby steps to deliver the ONE to the First Step class and then to the Second Step class. The goal for attendance is 20 percent of their AWA, which means 200 in total attendance if First Church is averaging 1,000 in AWA. The completion goal is set at 100 percent of those in attendance, along with the goal for group placements, serving placements, and new giving units. Through incredible effort and constant improvement, they are averaging a completion rate of nearly 80 percent.

SMALL GROUPS

Small Groups are First Church's chosen strategy for Piston 2 (Life-Changing Relationships). They have no other dedicated discipleship venue focused on relationships other than groups. They are firm believers that life change best happens in the context of relationship, so they give tremendous energy to this strategy, along with strong leadership. Even so, they know the key to meeting goals for small groups is an effective Engagement Pathway built with a strong ONE-aware filter. The ONE might want and need Life-Changing Relationships, but helping them build those relationships can be a challenge.

First Church defines a small group as a known and sponsored group of people of no less than two and no more than twenty, with an endorsed and trained First Church leader. The Small Group must meet at least twice monthly on average and remain accountable to First Church coaches, staff, and leaders. First Church has dedicated small groups for students and adults of many types.

The primary means for connecting the ONE to a small group is the Second Step class. There is an ever-present small group booth in the lobby for those who have questions or want to find a group. First Church also has a periodic emphasis from the platform, special seasons for connection events, and even church-wide campaigns that are effective for onboarding new group members and giving the ONE a short-term group trial experience.

First Church Small Group Measurables and Goals

The measurables for small groups are group members, number of groups, group leaders, and group apprentice leaders. Again, First Church sets a high bar by expecting their baby steps to deliver the ONE to the First Step and Second Step classes and then connect the ONE to a small group. The goal for the number of members in small groups is 80 percent of their AWA. If First Church is averaging 1,000 in AWA, the team expects 800 to be committed to a dedicated small group. This is a huge goal! (And it's been the hardest goal to hit.) But remember, First Church's audience of those who call it home is probably closer to 3,000 people. The total number of groups is the number of members divided by 10 (or more), which means they want 80 or more groups so the groups are no larger than 10 members. The goal for leaders and apprentices is equal to the total number of groups, and the goal for coaches (leaders of leaders) is one coach for every ten groups.

SERVE / GIVE / SHARE

At First Church, serving is a way for each person to use her or his gifts and to find a place of meaningful contribution. Giving and sharing your faith are also expected outflows of progressive commitment. They represent Piston 3 (Surrendered Living) of the Great Commission Engine and are key to First Church's plan to double its kingdom impact. First Church realizes the Engagement Pathway is going to deliver the beginning opportunities for gift-based service, onboarding new givers, and encouraging people to share their faith. It's in the application of these things that God will grow those committed to him as well as First Church.

First things first, though. You must define serving, giving, and sharing in a way each can be measured. First Church had to decide what a serving opportunity was, and then create some rules around it in order to count it. A serving slot at First Church is a known and defined slot that requires at least one hour of service per month. These serving slots are known, defined, and captured by the team so they can know if the slot is filled or not, and if so, by whom. Furthermore, First Church doesn't count the same person twice if they are filling two slots—they are counted only once.

The primary means for connecting the ONE and others to a serving slot is the Second Step class, the same as for small groups. There is an ever-present enlistment booth in the lobby for those who have questions or want to find a spot. First Church also has a periodic emphasis from the platform, special seasons for connection events, and even church-wide campaigns focused on serving. Serving is an area where First Church pays special attention to honoring the simple-step design so the ONE (and anyone else) doesn't get slotted or committed to a spot that doesn't make sense or isn't the right fit. All serving slot commitments are temporary until the ONE says it's the right fit.

Giving and sharing your faith are easy to understand, but one is more difficult to measure than the other. Giving is defined as the tithes and offerings of the church family, whether as an owner or not. Sharing is praying for, investing in, and inviting those who need Christ to church. First Church has embraced the language of the ONE, and everyone is asked to have at least a single ONE for whom they are praying. The expectation for owners is that they envision their entire circle of family, friends, and coworkers as their personal reach zone.

First Church Serve / Give / Share Measurables and Goals

The measurable for serving is the total number of servants or volunteers. First Church sets a high bar by expecting their baby steps to deliver the ONE to the First Step class and then the Second Step class. Second Step is built to make these commitments simple for the ONE and anyone in attendance. The goal for the number of servants is a minimum of 40 percent of the AWA. If First Church's AWA is 1,000, the team expects a minimum of 400 dedicated servants in a dedicated slot (counted once). This is a huge goal, and it's been the second most difficult goal to hit. But First Church's true audience is closer to 3,000 people. Corporate giving and sharing goals have yet to be set outside of the onboarding goals discussed in the Second Step section and normal budgeting cycles.

CORE

First Church calls its core-committed church members *owners*. (We spoke about the definition of owners earlier.) First Church knows if they can build a dedicated core group, they will have an army that is on mission with them. The base commitments of ownership are serving, giving, sharing, and group participation. If anyone makes these commitments, God will change his or her life. The core of owners is depicted at the bottom of the funnel, but this is only the beginning of deep engagement. A dedicated core group is required to drive double kingdom impact, and the Engagement Pathway must move people to this level of commitment.

One word about church membership vs. core vs. owner: With this concept, you catch the vision of an ignited core group who is on mission with you. Owners at First Church are effectively parallel to what some churches call membership. Perhaps you have a roll of members and a membership process. In some cases, formal membership is required for voting and such. So, if *core* equals *member* to you, that's great. Just remember what the core looks like and how they act. We've explained to many churches that not all members are in your core, and some of your core are not members. You probably have more core people than you know. A healthy exercise could be to define what your base commitment is for your version of ownership and make a list of people. Set a date and have a rally about double kingdom impact!

First Church Owner Measurables and Goals

The measurable for owners is the total number of commitments. First Church expects their baby steps to deliver the ONE to the First Step and Second Step classes. The Second Step class is designed to make ownership commitments simple for the ONE and anyone in attendance. The goal for the number of owners is a minimum of 25 percent of the AWA. If First Church averages 1,000 in AWA, the team expects a minimum of 250 dedicated owners. First Church believes if it can build this base, it can ignite its reach zone like never before.

A SUMMARY OF MEASUREMENTS

Here's a recap of the First Church Engagement Pathway and the measurable goals for each part of the funnel, which First Church believes will drive double kingdom impact:

Engagement Pathway	Measurable	Goal
Weekend Worship Service	Average weekend attendance (AWA)	Grow by 15 percent annually
Baby Steps	Baby steps taken	100% of AWA (annually)
First Step Class	Attendance	20% of AWA (annually)
	Completion	100%
	Salvations	32–50% of class attendance
Conversion / Baptism	Baptisms	20% of AWA (annually)
Second Step Class	Attendance	100% of AWA (annually)
	Group starts	100% of class
	Serve starts	100% of class
	Giving starts	100% of class
Small Groups	Group members	80% of AWA
	Expected # of groups	Group membership/10
	Coaches	Total groups/10
	Leaders	100% of # of groups
	Apprentice leaders	100% of # of groups
Serve / Give / Share	Servants	40+% of AWA
Core	Owners	25% of AWA

We're not suggesting you copy this Engagement Pathway, but we want you to learn from it and get to work on your own. Here are some quick tips to help.

10 Quick Tips for Implementation

1. WORK FROM THE TOP OF THE FUNNEL TO THE BOTTOM. If the top isn't working well, it doesn't matter how the bottom works. The early stage connections matter the most.

2. KEEP IT SIMPLE. We've seen all kinds of designs and many are too complex. Don't overthink it, and don't try to make everything you have fit or pick five points of entry into the funnel. One simple pathway is best to begin with.

3. EXPERIMENT WITH EARLY SIMPLE STEPS (the baby steps in our example). The top of the funnel is the most important. Try a few things, test them, and adjust them. There is also space in the funnel where you can get ideas from other churches. Many are experimenting with early stage connection methods. It won't be hard to find options.

4. PLUG IN EXISTING MINISTRIES, CLASSES, ETC. There is no need to start at square one if you have a few things that are working well or appear to have potential. For instance, if pizza with the pastor has been working for you, just put the ONE-aware filter on it and plug it into the pathway in the right spot.

5. GET RID OF THE INFORMATION DESK AND THE PAMPHLETS. These give the ONE a transactional feel, and you want to move to a *relational* feel. You should also move to a full-service mind-set where those who staff these areas operate more like concierges than directory assistance operators.

6. ASSESS YOUR ENGAGEMENT PATHWAY ROUTINELY AND INCREMENTALLY IMPROVE IT. Four Helpful Lists should be used routinely on your Engagement Pathway. Once you've discovered something to leverage or issues to address, be aggressive. Have a sense of urgency. You will be surprised when you tweak something and get an immediate breakthrough.

7. SET THE BAR HIGH TO DRIVE DOUBLE KINGDOM IMPACT. This will take time, but double kingdom impact is, in some ways, just a math

problem. If you want to grow by 15 percent annually and you're losing people instead, you must connect with new people (preferably mostly ONEs) and pivot them to join mission with you and Jesus.

8. BE PATIENT. We alluded to it in our example. Building an effective Engagement Pathway takes time—more than you expect. Furthermore, you're never going to be done assessing it and making adjustments. First Church and many others have been working on their pathway for years!

9. BUILD IT FOR YOUR ONE. Above all else, start with the ONE and build the pathway back toward you. Don't start with you and your church and try to build a pathway to the ONE, because you will end up making it all about you.

10. DON'T WORRY TOO MUCH ABOUT THE NINETY-NINE; THEY'LL FIGURE IT OUT.

We have seen Engagement Pathways work in hundreds of churches, so it can definitely work for your church. When you make it easy to follow and highly visible, people will want to get onboard and take the steps. When they do, movement happens organically from the Relational Reach Zone, through the early steps to committed followers, to becoming part of your Ninety-Nine. We anticipate great things as you design and implement your own Engagement Pathway!

Intentional Churches have a stated and measured method to connect the ONE to the church, Christ, and others. They realize it is key to the Great Commission Engine running well and driving double kingdom impact.

Now that you have the ONE design and the Engagement Pathway to connect with them, it's time to address your vision for double kingdom impact. Your future is meant to be the outflow that connects your ONE to you, Jesus, and others.

AN ONLINE ENGAGEMENT PATHWAY

THE CROSSING CHURCH—LAS VEGAS, NEVADA

Scott Whaley

What does it look like to have a weekend experience that is online and in demand in today's world? If our weekend experience with our ONE were online, we would be asking what our Engagement Pathway looks like online. Is there a different digital pathway?

On social media we published a baptism photo of twentysomething Ryan baptizing a friend. Cameron saw this and was intrigued. Ryan is a physical trainer, and so Cameron wrote to him: "I want to get more positive stuff in my life. Maybe I could start training with you?" Under the value of rich community, Ryan set up an appointment with Cameron at the same time that he had an appointment with one of our staff, Josiah. So these three begin to build a relationship while training.

Ryan and Josiah regularly invited Cameron to church, but Cameron politely declined. Then Cameron had a life experience and came to our At the Movies series. He came back for several weeks and eventually became involved in a small group. When it came time for Easter baptisms, Cameron sought out Josiah and said, "I'm not getting baptized yet, because I want to get baptized next month when my parents come to visit on the day my sister died of a drug overdose." Josiah set up a special baptism and redeemed that day for Cameron and his family.

THE BIG DEAL ABOUT BABY STEPS

WEST SIDE CHRISTIAN CHURCH—SPRINGFIELD, ILLINOIS

Melissa Sandel

While we were working with Intentional Churches, we learned the importance of taking baby steps. We created an entire Engagement Pathway team that works together, and each member has a specialty. We ask people to take small steps and drive for movement quickly. As a result, we have seen an acceleration in people getting involved.

We have moved our "New to West Side" booth to the open area near the main entrance. It is more obvious and less intimidating to visit. The only thing people hear about when they are in that space is an invitation to First Step, which is a monthly forty-five-minute crash course on a Sunday morning, with donuts and coffee. It's more like a celebration. The primary messages people hear at First Steps are:

- The importance of coming to worship and bringing a friend.
- Ten quick tips for newcomers covering some logistics and making sense of the experience at West Side. We do this in a fun way.
- An invitation to join a Rooted Group.

Rooted is a discipleship group tool we push. It not only gives people a discipleship and community experience, but it teaches them missional living. So it transitions people from rich community into missional living and giving.

People, especially our ONE, need a simple, easily understood process and not something overwhelming. If we overcomplicate it, people are paralyzed and can't make a decision on following Jesus and getting involved in the church.

For more stories and case studies, please visit
www.intentionalchurches.com.

EIGHT

DOUBLE VISION: THE TENSION OF TRUE NORTH

And the Lord answered me:

"Write the vision;

make it plain on tablets,

so he may run who reads it."

—HABAKKUK 2:2 ESV

Bob Goff is an attorney, speaker, and bestselling author who shares a story about a sailing trip and the idea of true north. One day he was asked to be the navigator, even though he was an amateur sailor at best. Here's the essence of that story:

This would be the longest trip I had ever undertaken as a sailor. I went to my home marina and asked for some maps, to which the professionals selling me the maps promptly replied, "You mean *charts*?" Something told me I was in trouble!

I put the chart on a table and plotted a direct line from my marina to Diamond Head, Hawaii. I packed my supplies and decided to have a friend check out my chart to make sure I wouldn't get lost. Boy, am I glad I did!

His first question, after making a bit of fun of my straight-line path to Hawaii, was, "Are you going to navigate by true north or magnetic north?" I had no clue what he was talking about!

He went on to explain that true north is based on the North Pole, which is a fixed position. Magnetic north is not fixed and varies based on the earth's magnetic fields. It shifts based on where you are on the planet.

Evidently, the difference is greater when traveling long distances. If you are navigating from your seat in the parking lot, the difference wouldn't matter all that much. But if you are traveling from California to Hawaii, you could miss the entire island chain![1]

Bob's story is informative for your church. Your heading, not your instruments or your measurements, will always determine your destination. In the short term, it may not make that big of a difference, but in the long term, slight adjustments early on will cause major missteps later, as well as missing your target. There is nothing more powerful than determining your church's true north. What compass heading will determine your direction? Are you looking for a magnetic north that shifts and changes over time? Or will it be an unchanging, unwavering true north?

We cannot overstate how important this is. We've already discussed the silver-bullet mentality, lack of a common rubric for decision-making, and the tendency toward poor evaluation methods. One of the best ways to neutralize all of those common challenges is to establish a true north as a team. Where is God leading you? What will get you there? What won't? Is your current ministry performance (component by component) in a position to drive you toward your true north? These questions are paramount to ChurchOS.

We believe a future vision of double kingdom impact can create a true north for your church. Double vision is best discerned when you are at an altitude above your ministry and can clearly see both realities of today's and tomorrow's horizon.

WHAT IS VISION?

You could ask a dozen church leaders to define *vision* and you would get fifteen different answers. Church vision statements vary greatly as well. They range from pie-in-the-sky aspirational statements to single words that recap the essence of the Great Commission, the church's given mission. Church vision is a confusing topic, but it doesn't have to be.

First, here are a few things the Bible has to say about vision.

The most quoted verse about vision is Proverbs 29:18. The old King James Version is easily remembered: "Where there is no vision, the people perish." In the New Living Translation, the word is translated "divine guidance," and we think that is very accurate. Vision is the guidance from God for you right where and when you are.

Vision is very personal. The apostle Paul had a personal vision for his ministry, outlined in Acts 9:15. He was called to be an apostle to the Gentiles, which is a specific vision he was able to see only after God changed his heart.

But vision must also be the result of passion. When Nehemiah heard about the destruction of the walls of Jerusalem, he sat down and wept (Neh. 1:4). But that led him to prayer, and prayer led to vision. God put a plan in his heart (2:12) that he was able to communicate to the Persian king, Artaxerxes (2:5–8). Vision is passion that leads to planning.

Finally, Jesus himself was given a vision. Luke 4:14–30 outlines his own plan to proclaim good news to the poor, freedom to prisoners, recovery of sight for the blind, and to set the oppressed free (v. 18). But how would he accomplish all of that? Mark 10:45 gives us the answer: to lay down his life as a servant rather than be served.

The Bible is clear about the importance of vision and its power. Vision always includes a keen sense of today's truth, hope for the future, and a realistic idea of the work that lies ahead.

Here is our definition of vision when it comes to the local church:

Vision is a God-born, clear, and compelling description of the preferred future for your church. It is the result of Great Commission activation.

Here are some characteristics of a great local church vision:

TRANSFORMATION: It always includes a picture of changed lives and the difference Christ makes, especially in the life of your ONE.

THE RIPPLE EFFECT: It anticipates the downline impact of lives being changed and what will happen in your church, your community, your region, and beyond.

QUANTITATIVE AND QUALITATIVE: It contains descriptive statements about your future but also the objective and measurable aspects of your future.

UNDERSTANDABLE AND REPEATABLE: The Ninety-Nine can grasp it and repeat it in their own words. Refer back to Gene Appel's story in chapter 2.

ASPIRATIONAL AND INSPIRATIONAL: It elevates thinking, gives hope, and breathes life into those connected to it. It is the why!

RESULT OF GREAT COMMISSION ACTIVATION: Your vision is the future result of your accomplishment of Christ's mission over time.

DOUBLE VISION: A NEW TRUE NORTH

We believe one of the primary purposes of vision is to create healthy tension, that is, a sense of the possible only if God helps us. Tension can be a healthy and very useful thing. Proper tension creates strength, informs direction, and unifies. Proper tension is very helpful.

In the American Southwest, most of our homes are built on concrete slabs. These slabs have cables running from one side to the other and are tightened to maintain a certain pressure. This tensioning system allows the slab to remain intact when the weather changes and when the ground shifts. Without this tension, major cracks form in the foundation of the house. It's a great example of how pressure and tension can be usefully applied.

Another example for how vision creates healthy and directional tension is to think of a rubber band stretched between two hands. As you pull your hands apart, the rubber band stretches. When you bring them together, the rubber band goes slack. Think of one hand as representing today and the other as representing tomorrow. Great vision acts nearly the same way. It puts tension on your plans and activities. It informs direction. Just like the rubber band, too much tension will break it. The same is true for a pie-in-the-sky vision that isn't believable. It doesn't really inform our next steps or pull us toward tomorrow with direction. Vision that is too shallow or weak will not inform direction just as a slack rubber band doesn't do much between your hands. There is no built-up energy or useful tension to instruct the next steps. It also allows you to wander aimlessly, maybe moving forward, maybe not. The art of good visioning is like stretching a rubber band between your hands just enough, without breaking, but your hands can do little more than move directly toward each other.

We believe the frame of double vision does just this: it places informative, directional, and proper tension on our plans. Furthermore, we believe most churches can achieve double vision in five years or less, once they are growing at a regular pace. Doubling your impact in five years means about 15 percent growth compounding year after year. That is a stretch to achieve and sustain for sure, but we've seen it happen again and again. We believe it's the gold standard for church visioning. As you already know, we use double kingdom impact as our ChurchOS standard when setting expectations for tomorrow.

So why is double kingdom vision our frame?

- SEEING DOUBLE: Double isn't crazy. Double is within reach. We can all see it. Our churches are typically filled with people at Christmas and Easter. We can see what it's like to have a full house. We can see the dynamics in children's areas, parking lots, and worship spaces. We can anticipate the challenges that double would bring and, conversely, what strategies might unlock our double potential. No matter where you've been or where you are today, double seems possible if you let yourself dream a bit!

- DOUBLE VISION IS INSPIRING AND LIFE GIVING: In Proverbs 29:18, Solomon told us, "When people do not accept divine guidance, they run wild," right? Double impact means growing. And growing is a righteous pursuit in church and in life. We were born to grow. We were made to grow. It's why running a mile can inspire you to run two, and two miles can inspire you to aspire to a half-marathon one day. If you're blessed with ability, you might even run a marathon! When we are on the pursuit to double, we are truly living.

- DOUBLE VISION CATALYZES A CLEAR RESPONSE: When you clarify vision, you learn a lot about who's with you and who's sitting on the sidelines. I remember the first time I (Bart) experienced the call to join in the planning to double Central's impact. Honestly, it was a serious and significant gut check, because I was exhausted from our just-completed relocation effort. At first I wasn't sure I was ready to jump in and do my part. But it wasn't long until I knew I wanted to be all in. Too much was at stake. What else could I do but say, "I'm in"?

- DOUBLE VISION ALIGNS YOUR TEAM: We are all better off when we know where we are headed and how our individual contributions matter. If you're like us, you don't want to micromanage your team's actions. You want them to lead themselves and make decisions as you do. A simple way to do this is to clarify the vision again and again. You've probably heard, "Vision leaks." Reframing the why in clear terms on a regular basis will help your team and culture more than you know.

- DOUBLE VISION CLARIFIES STRATEGY: If you are clear and honest about your current situation, then an immediate gap is formed between today and your vision to double. It's in this gap the how becomes clear. Not only does strategy become clearer, but you begin to develop an immediate sense of priority. What must be done now? What must be done next? The answers to those elusive questions are much easier when the vision is clear.

- DOUBLE VISION LEADS TO BREAKTHROUGH THINKING: Achieving double impact will almost always require innovation and new thinking, regardless of your environment. You will have to stretch and work hard as a team. With the salient question in front of you, "What must be true to double our impact?" you will begin to clearly see the areas that need to be addressed. What has helped you achieve your current or past success likely won't lead to Great Commission activation in the future. You've probably heard these phrases, "What got us here won't get us there" or "Today's solution is tomorrow's challenge." This is true when you dream and plan for double kingdom impact. A consistently refreshed vision for double kingdom impact will change you and your team in a good way.

Here's a quick tip. Don't allow questions that can stifle responses, such as "How much will this cost?" or "We are already overtaxed as a team. How are we going to find room in our schedule or budget for this?" These questions can come later. Use the "what must be true" paradigm to lead you to answers, even if those answers or ideas are audacious at first. Due diligence on the ideas will come later.

We consider double kingdom vision the true north and the minimum standard for your church. It should be the primary point for navigation and course correction. It will stretch you like never before. It should become central to your evaluation and planning. We know some churches that dreamed even bigger and shortened the time frame from five years to three. Regardless, the principle works the same. Stretch out your vision however far you need to in order to create the kind of tension that leads to courageous action and breakthrough thinking, the change that leads to increased gospel impact.

WHAT IS DOUBLE KINGDOM VISION?

Double kingdom vision is the result of activating the Great Commission (the making of more and better disciples). As the Great Commission Engine produces results, it transforms the ONE into a devoted follower of Jesus, placing them on mission with Christ and your church. The outflow of this transformation will become your future reality, your vision.

DOUBLE IMPACT IS QUALITATIVE AND QUANTITATIVE.

- QUALITATIVE VISION: These are estimations of future vision that can be stated in clear terms but might not necessarily be empirically measurable. Here are a few examples:
  - We are a sending center for future missionaries.
  - We are diminishing the drug epidemic and hunger issues in our county.
  - We are known for our culture of grace and friendliness and for allowing people to come as they are.
- QUANTITATIVE VISION: Some vision has numbers attached to it. Obviously, when you are thinking double, one of the easiest things to do is to put a vision together that has some metrics to it. For instance:
  - We are a church of 1,000 in average weekend attendance.
  - We have grown our base of elementary kids from 20 percent to 25 percent of our average attendance.
  - We have 400 people serving at least once a month at our church.

DOUBLE IMPACT INVOLVES EVERY COMPONENT OF THE GREAT COMMISSION ENGINE

Double kingdom vision requires all pistons to fire effectively. What is your five-year double (minimum) vision for each aspect of the GCE? What will be the qualitative and quantitative vision for each component?

DOUBLE IMPACT STARTS WITH THE IMPACT ON YOUR ONE AND THEN RIPPLES OUTWARD

Acts: 1:8 Impact Model

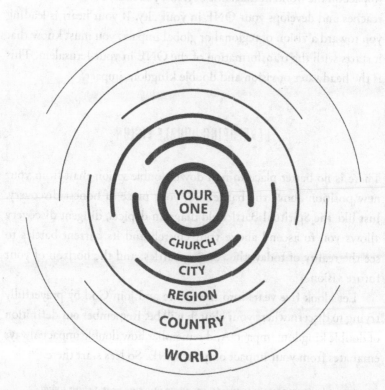

In Acts 1:8 we are given a model for kingdom impact. Jesus tells his followers they will be his witnesses in Jerusalem, Judea, Samaria, and the ends of the earth. We believe this simple model gives us great hints at prioritization and the source of kingdom impact. You must be impacting people in Jerusalem (your home), changing the lives of your ONE, in order to fuel a movement that impacts your city, your region, your country, and the world. It can also be said that if you do impact the ONE in your Jerusalem, you will make eternal ripples in your city, region, and the world. We're going to repeat what we've said before: you likely have no idea how many eternal ripples you've already made, regardless of the size or current condition of your church. To God be the glory!

This is so important. Please don't miss it. Impacting the world traces back to your impact on the ONE. If you want to have a great impact on the world in the name of Jesus, you must build a church that reaches and develops your ONE in your city. If your heart is leading you toward a vision of regional or global impact, you must know that it starts with the transformation of the ONE in your Jerusalem. This is the headwater of vision and double kingdom impact.

DEVELOPING DOUBLE VISION

There is no better place to nail down double vision than from your new position above the battlefield, your place of honest discovery. Just like the Spiritual Battlefield diagram depicts, diligent discovery allows you to ascend above your church and its current battles to see the reality of today, the coming battles, and the horizon of your future vision.

Let's look five years into the future and join God by prayerfully trying to discern where your church will be. Remember our definition of double kingdom impact. And remember how double impact always emanates from your impact on your ONE. So let's start there.

WHAT IS YOUR DEVELOPMENTAL VISION FOR YOUR ONE FIVE YEARS FROM NOW?

Think back a couple of chapters to how you defined your ONE, the central focus of ChurchOS and the Great Commission Engine. As a team, you've come to better understand the ONE, but now you want to join the ONE and God in the great transformation of the ONE's life. Let's envision how the ONE's life is different because of the work of your church. Here are a few questions to ask (take some notes).

- What do they know, love, and do now as a Christ follower?
- How have their values changed after they've come to know Jesus?

- How has their family changed and their life as a parent and spouse changed?
- What does their involvement look like at your church?
- What does their involvement look like in each of the GCE components?
- What does their daily routine look like? What habits have they formed?
- How do they view their career, gifts, and skills?
- How has their definition of fulfillment changed?

WHAT IS YOUR VISION FOR YOUR CHURCH FIVE YEARS FROM NOW?

Let's use the Great Commission Engine components to qualitatively and quantitatively dig in with a few visioning questions. You can refer back to the chapters on the GCE if you want to better understand the future of what should be happening. Let's take some more notes.

The ONE

- What is your plan to reach the ONE and constantly measure your culture of invitation?
- How many invites do you estimate are occurring?
- Is your church built and ready for the ONE? If so, how? Are you ready to change and adapt as needed?
- Are your Ninety-Nine on mission with you and trained in personal evangelism?

Piston I (Catalytic Weekend Experience)

- What does Piston 1 look like?
- How many are attending?
- What does the feel and structure of your services look like?
- What about the components of the weekend experience (parking, children's ministry, etc.)?

Piston 2 (Life-Changing Relationships)

- What does your strategy for Life-Changing Relationships look like?
- What is your strategy for building Life-Changing Relationships?
- How many are attending small groups?
- What does your leadership structure look like?
- How does your ONE find a small group and join it?

Piston 3 (Surrendered Living)

- What will Surrendered Living look like?
- How many will be serving?
- What is your plan for generosity?
- What is your per capita giving and plan to onboard new givers?

Engagement Pathway

- How is your Engagement Pathway performing?
- Are your baby steps and first steps working?
- How many have taken those steps?
- How many decisions for Christ has your Engagement Pathway produced?
- How many have connections to serving and groups?

FIVE YEARS FROM NOW, WHAT KIND OF ETERNAL RIPPLES ARE HAPPENING AS A RESULT OF YOUR MINISTRY IN YOUR CITY, REGION, AND BEYOND?

As you let your heart flow from your dream for the ONE to the dream for your church and beyond, a natural alignment should be forming. If double impact is happening in the life of your ONE and your church, you can begin to believe and hear from God about what will be happening in your city, region, and world. Here are a few pertinent visioning questions.

- How is your city different because of your church?
- What is your church known for in your town or county?
- How do others in your city or region describe your church?
- How is your ONE intersecting with your town at work, in the field, etc.?
- What kind of global influence do you have? How? Through what?

WRITE YOUR OWN "I HAVE A DREAM" SPEECH

Now, with your heart stirred and your mind's eye opened, write a single-page summary of your five-year vision. Remember some of the benchmarks of a great vision:

- Realistic but stretching
- Qualitative and quantitative
- Concrete and understandable
- Starts with the ONE
- Looks like Acts 1:8

Here's an example from Salty Church in Ormond Beach, Florida. Just think how this simple vision, agreed upon by the team, has led to courageous, strategic thinking and decisions.

In five years, Salty is running 2,800 on six campuses! The vision to start new campuses up and down the coast has come to fruition, and we have moved beyond our borders to partner with new churches around the world. We have walked to the Atlantic hundreds of times to baptize more than 1,000 new believers in Christ. Our believers are on mission with us to win our region to Christ. We have expanded our facilities and the growth is palpable. Our Invitation Culture is irresistible and has even newcomers bringing guests. Our Engagement Pathway is crystal clear on all campuses and consistently moving people toward their next step with Christ.

Groups have exploded due to clear on-ramps presented through intentional LifeGroup efforts, growing more disciples and leaders of disciples. Salty flourishes with stories of real-life change. Because of the generosity of our people, the community is known to say, "Call Salty, they will help with that!" Salty Family Services has helped over 300 families in five years. Our mission focus is to make more and better disciples, engage people, and reproduce leaders.

Salty has an inspiring vision. It is concrete but also stretches. It's measurable and descriptive. Writing out your vision may come naturally to you or it might not. Don't get hung up on this. There is no perfect vision description. (We feature variations on our blog from time to time.) Some descriptions use inspiring language in the style of Martin Luther King Jr. Others are pragmatic and contain numbers, goals, and concrete future realities. So you need to write one and distribute it to your leadership team. Start working on it now.

Here are a couple of tips. First, use your team to sort through a long list of five-year vision thoughts. Distribute the questions above in a single document to the team. Next, assign an editor to pull everyone's thoughts together. If you've been following the ChurchOS process, you will be amazed at the similarity of your five-year dreams. If you are the senior pastor, you may want to be the editor, and of course you will want the final say on the vision description. Finally, if you have a hard time writing out your description, write a paragraph or two and read it every morning for a week or two. You will see God highlight portions of it and expand your thinking. He will help you to refine your vision!

VISION IN ITS FULLEST FORM

As you begin to communicate the vision to others and use it as tensioning device, you will find that the full vision is born from great discovery. Vision that leads people into action and helps them discern the next steps is inspiring, based in reality, and contains a sense of what is to come. As you develop your visioning skills as a team and use the Intentional Growth Planning process, you will begin to think this way naturally. As a leader, you will let people know that you understand the truth of your current situation, where God is leading you, and what you should be focused on and what must be done.

Earlier we pointed to the visionary leadership of Nehemiah, which was fueled by both passion and a plan. He was also able to cast his vision based on honest discovery. The reality of his day led him to his knees in tears and prayer. But it also sparked something else, namely, a vision for how Jerusalem could be. He saw beyond the state of exile and bondage to freedom. He also knew there would be battles ahead, and he prepared for them. Just approaching the Persian king was risky, but he needed Artaxerxes' resources to tackle the tasks before him. He also knew he would face rejection and opposition when he arrived in Judea. Finally, he put all those things in perspective when he pictured a brighter future, one where the city walls were rebuilt, the gates restored, and the people of the land revived! Nehemiah was a leader who understood full vision.

MAINTAINING DOUBLE VISION

ROLLING VISION CYCLES

Vision is dynamic, but one of the mistakes we see leaders make occurs when their vision is too static. We don't believe in determining your five-year vision and then waiting five years to refresh it. We tell leadership teams, "Hold it loosely, but take it seriously." Why? God gave you the initial vision, *and* he can do immeasurably more than you can hope or dream. You will also inevitably advance your church forward, which means your vision horizon will shift as well as your current circumstances. You should expect to repeat the cycle of Intentional

Growth Planning periodically, which includes redesigning your vision expectations and resetting your picture of double kingdom impact.

If you begin to grow at a 15 percent pace annually, you should expect to refresh your five-year vision no less than yearly. If you are growing at a slower rate, you can expect to refresh your vision every one or two years. Those growing faster may find themselves needing to renew the vision every few months. If you are getting fuzzy or unclear about your next steps, it's possible the vision has lost focus. The healthy tension is gone. It's time for a refresh.

VISIONING IS LIKE A MUSCLE YOU DEVELOP IN TIME

As you repeat the Intentional Growth Planning cycle, it will become more natural and intuitive to you. You will pick up the pace and develop an ability to go through the phases quickly. This includes visioning. It will become second nature and intuitive for the whole team, especially if you routinely involve them in the effort. Your vision will get clearer, specific, inspiring, and detailed. It will become like a cloud-shared document that is constantly being updated and edited by you and the team.

Early in the book, I (Bart) mentioned a story of incredible impact when we baptized more than twelve hundred people one weekend. I'm convinced that day would have never happened if we had not adopted the principles and cycles in this book. We kept ourselves under healthy vision tension. We often asked ourselves, "What would it look like for Central to double its kingdom impact?" Then we lined out the next season's work and got after it.

Not long ago Central rolled out the next double kingdom vision to the congregation. The creative graphic they used is on the next page.

We love this picture for many reasons. Yes, it's full of numbers, but it's also full of statements and inspiring imagery. It tells you exactly what the leaders are expecting and what Central, as a church, is fighting for. It represents true north for this body of Christ in the next season.

You can see and feel it.

It is inspiring and life giving.

It catalyzes a clear response.

It aligns the team and the whole church.

It is strategically clear.

It leads to courageous next steps and decisions.

What's your true north?

Intentional Churches use a clear vision of double kingdom impact to inspire and inform their decisions. They refresh and communicate it often to create ownership, healthy tension, and alignment.

CHANGE MANAGEMENT

FIRST CHRISTIAN CHURCH—MORRIS, ILLINOIS

Scott Zorn and Todd Thomson

Once we identified our ONE, we realized our weekend experience was totally missing that person. That was a surprise to us and became a top priority. Our ONE is forty-year-old J.D. He's a former Catholic, and his kids are involved in activities. His wife would like the kids to come to church, but she won't overstep J.D.'s boundaries. A woman in our group described him perfectly because J.D. was just like all her husband's friends.

Our weekend experiences were doing the opposite of what we wanted them to do to meet J.D. Honestly, the changes we needed were painful. One of these included our entire worship environment. We were in a round, antiquated, limited-seating sanctuary with pews. As we started talking about the environment we needed, one of the elders excitedly said, "We have a gym! Why aren't we going in there!?"

He was right. We already had the space we were describing. We just needed to transform it. It was a big decision to flip the building, and we lost some people over it, as well as a staffing change we made. But all along the way, we kept seeing God move as we cast the vision.

One of the biggest vision-casting moments for me (Scott) was with a group called the Dorcas Quilters. I don't know what got into me. (God must have.) I just decided I would spend an hour every Tuesday with these ladies, even though they had a reputation of complaining at times. While I was there, we had all kinds of cultural and generational conversations while they quilted. I said, "Ladies, I am going to let you in on something I have not even asked the elders about yet. We are thinking about getting rid of the pews and going to chairs. To my shock, they said, "Try it! Why not! Sounds good."

Our leaders went to every small group and talked about the vision, the reasons to make the move, and the ONE. It was a lot of groundwork, with hours and hours going face-to-face with all of them. The miraculous thing was that when we went to all the small groups, we were honest in saying we needed $20,000 for new chairs, but we didn't ask for any money when we talked to them. Well, we had the money before any announcement was ever made to the congregation. We also had some incredible people who transformed the gym into a worship center. Now, we find our younger people are inviting their friends!

Our strategy for managing change has been very relational. This experience has taught me (Scott) the difference between maintenance and real ministry. I could have maintained this pretty easily, kept the boat afloat. But now, lives are being changed. Now, I am leading people rather than leading a church.

LEANING ON THE COLLABORATIVE PROCESS

FIRST CHURCH—BURLINGTON, KENTUCKY

Tommy Baker

Our lead pastor had only been in his role for a short time when we started Intentional Growth Planning. We brought Intentional Churches in to help with his start. Although he had been a staff member for fifteen years and was a known commodity, this was his first time in a lead pastor role. Coming into that season of leadership and getting direction, while being very collaborative, allowed him to not just tell everyone where the train was going. We could lean into the process to exact a bit of change collaboratively instead of having one person direct it. We had staff, elders, and people from the congregation go through the process, and we had a lot of stakeholder buy-in.

The process also fostered creativity. If you tell me where you want to go, and then tell me how I need to get there, then you don't need me. Just do it yourself. But creativity and ownership come when you talk about where you want to go together and when everyone is involved in creating the path to get there.

For more stories and case studies, please visit
www.intentionalchurches.com.

The Intentional Growth Planning core process of ChurchOS includes four phases: discover, design, organize, and activate. You have ascended above the battlefield to discern the truth of today's battle. You have designed the key elements of your battle plan. Now it's time to organize your team around key Vision Initiative Projects while looking at tomorrow's challenges and your ultimate vision. This phase is critical because the job of the church leader is to determine priorities and to keep the team focused while descending back to the battle. It also emphasizes the importance of cross-ministry work groups working with your traditional organizational chart to produce double kingdom impact.

Intentional Growth Planning™ (IGP)

Applying the ChurchOS
Living Toolbox™

1 DISCOVER   DESIGN 2

YOUR CHURCH
Great Commission Engine™
& Double Vision

ACTIVATE   ORGANIZE
4   3

NINE

VISIONARY DECISIONS

I planted the seed in your hearts, and Apollos watered it, but it was God who made it grow. It's not important who does the planting, or who does the watering. What's important is that God makes the seed grow.

—1 CORINTHIANS 3:6–7

I f you honor the many phases of disciplined discovery and careful design, the next season's work will emerge quite naturally. You have ascended above the thick of the battle to discover the true nature of your current circumstances. You have lifted your head to the horizon and carefully thought through your ONE and Engagement Pathway—two core strategies every church must design. Now, in the healthy tension of the gap between these strategies, you can begin the process of discerning your next season's work.

This work is where you partner with God in leading your church. Remember, the power of the gospel is infinite, and we serve a sovereign, all-knowing, and all-powerful God. He invites us into this partnership through the Great Commission. He is the one who will grow your church, but he will use your efforts in combination with his sovereignty to do so. You will activate the Great Commission, and he will release the gospel potential of your church.

TWO TYPES OF EFFORT

To grow your church, you must put two types of effort into it: today effort and tomorrow effort. It's at the intersection of these efforts that double kingdom impact emerges. Here's a diagram to help you understand what we mean.

WHAT IS TODAY EFFORT?

This is the near-term energy you put into the structure of your church. It represents your organizational chart, roles, and job descriptions. It is your Tuesday staff meeting, the upcoming lunch you have with a key volunteer, and the next teaching series you have planned. It represents the Sunday that is coming and the fifty-two that will follow it. A book titled *It's Friday, but Sunday's Coming* appeared in 1984, and those words are an undeniable truth for church leaders![1] Most teams are up to their eyeballs in their day-to-day work. They use every ounce of resources they have and then some. But eternity is at stake. The weight of today feels heavy to most church leaders. Does it feel that way to you?

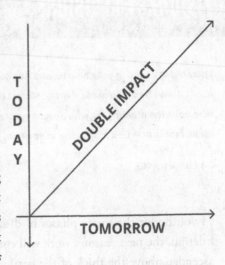

WHAT IS TOMORROW EFFORT?

This is the energy we put into strategic projects and growth-oriented planning and systems. Unfortunately, it's a rarity to find this type of energy in some churches. Yet it is such a necessary asset! Today and tomorrow effort both are vital to create a trajectory toward double impact, just as the illustration depicts. If you expend only today effort, you'll do what is necessary, but that may not truly fulfill your vision. If you spend all your time strategizing or trying new things, you may sacrifice excellence and near-term effectiveness and not fulfill your vision as well. This is an important aspect of ChurchOS. It is built to help you stay clear and honest about today's work and blend it with the work that will advance you.

CHALLENGE #1

This is the number-one challenge as we head into getting organized for action, but it's also what makes getting and staying organized as a church leadership team very difficult. Inevitably, the dominance of the fifty-two-week rhythm takes over, and the tomorrow effort is minimalized, diminished, or, worse, abandoned. We've seen it and maybe you have experienced it. Not this time! Right?

Fifty years ago Charles Hummel tapped into one aspect of why businesses fail to be successful. In *Freedom from Tyranny of the Urgent* he outlined how what is important will clash with what is urgent.[2] The urgent will always win out. You know this as a pastor, sitting down to study for Sunday's message, when a text pops up about a flooded restroom or a member in need. The urgent immediately takes precedent over the important. That's what happens when we allow today effort to overshadow tomorrow effort.

There's another issue that adds to this challenge. You want to get and stay organized today but not at the sacrifice of tomorrow's vision. Vice versa, you don't want to be so focused on tomorrow that you sacrifice excellence in the near term. If you lean too far to one side or the other, you will definitely get stuck, retreat, and eventually not grow.

What can you do? How do you find the right balance for your church?

In ChurchOS, we found the most effective tool to be what we call Vision Initiative Projects (VIPs), which are organized around your church's next big growth initiative.

We are about to walk you through the formation of Vision

Initiative Projects (VIPs) that will be organized around your church's next big growth initiative. We are huge proponents of cross-ministry work groups being used constantly at your church to execute your mission and plan for double kingdom impact. These work groups have a tomorrow focus with a today agenda that must be blended with your existing near-term efforts. If you can form them, accomplish the objective, and remove the barrier that led to their formation, you will see the kingdom potential of your church released.

CHALLENGE #2

That leads us to the number-two challenge: making decisions as a team. Maybe you have this challenge, maybe you don't. We encourage you to lean into our process to discern your VIPs. You should use your planning team to help with the discernment. Remember, old-style leadership sent the senior leader to the mountain to hear from God so we knew what to do next. Now, we are going to discern this as a team while we listen closely to God's and our senior leaders' thoughts and direction.

So how do you discern this work?

THE LONG LIST

First, you make a list. Remember, VIPs live in the land between today and tomorrow (double vision). Use this to identify and prioritize them. To use the analogy, from your position over the battlefield through discovery and design, you can better spot what's coming and in what sequence.

VIP TEAM DEFINED (CROSS-MINISTRY WORK GROUP)

We have found it helpful to have a simple description of what a VIP team is *before* you start to make a list. Here are some simple criteria for a VIP:

- **SCOPE:** A VIP is a big project, not an action item. For instance, painting the wall in the lobby is a to-do; overhauling the facility is a VIP.
- **SIZE:** A VIP will require a team to accomplish the task. It's not a job for one or two people, but four to eight or even more. The project is big enough to break into smaller parts and needs several participants at each phase.
- **DURATION:** A VIP is going to take a while to accomplish. Sometimes you can knock out the objective in a few weeks, but we have seen some VIPs last for up to two years.
- **PURPOSE:** A VIP is *not* a research and development work group or only looking to make recommendations. VIPs are formed to accomplish an objective and assist in the removal of a barrier. They stay in place until the impact of their work is completed.
- **ACTION:** A VIP is *not* a traditional committee! A VIP is a work group specifically formed to take strategic action. It has a limited life span. It may exist for a month or longer, but eventually it disbands when its objective is met and its team members are redeployed to other VIPs.

These criteria should help you begin to narrow in on the emerging work. What kind of work in front of you looks like this? Here's a hint: In all our work to date, with thousands of VIPs formed, we have seen the following topics make the list. Each topic can be traced back to an effective Great Commission Engine and the Six Domains of Church.

- Weekend experience / worship experience
- Evangelism / culture of invitation
- Engagement Pathway / next steps / connections / assimilation
- The ONE identification and motivations
- Vision clarity / vision communication
- Volunteers / serving / activating ownership
- Leadership development

- Staff development / culture / health / alignment
- Communications internal / external / web / social
- Small groups / Sunday school / ABF
- Discipleship systems / pathway
- Long-range planning / facilities and funding
- Next Gen ministry / family / children / student
- Finances / stewardship / generosity
- Governance / elder and staff roles / decision-making
- Hiring / HR / reorganization / restructure
- Ministry prioritization / cleaning up the buffet
- Multisite strategy / multisite launch or strategy clean up
- Administrative systems / database
- Local outreach / missions
- Succession / transition planning

VIP DISCERNMENT

The only way to determine what is in your next season of work is to review the notes and summary work from discovery and design. Look back through your notes from your battlefield survey using the Great Commission Engine (Part 2). Review your evaluation and notes from a look at your top resource priorities. Finally, look through your notes from the three design elements of the ONE, the Engagement Pathway, and double kingdom impact. Pray and seek wisdom. What is God saying should be on your list?

Remember, you are only making a list, so it's okay to have several possibilities rise to the top. We typically let every member weigh in with what they believe are the emerging VIPs. A few things will happen when you have so much input. Primary among these, you will notice the alignment of your team. That's the power of the unified simple dialogue of ChurchOS. Not everything from our list above will make your list, which means you are converging on a short list of what the vision tension gap is that we've been talking about. You also will feel the weight of the work and the need to prioritize.

PRIORITIZING AND CHOOSING VIPS

Here is our method to seek the weighted wisdom of the team in prioritizing. You should have a list of possible VIPs at this point. Typically, most teams will develop a list of two to ten possibilities for the coming season. Make a list similar to the one we have here on a whiteboard, easel pad, or in your journal.

	VIP Long List

Here is the simple method we have seen work well. Some call it *stack ranking*. You are going to prioritize the list as a team, and here are your instructions.

- Each team member must rank the complete VIP long list on their own, meaning you make a ranked list from most important to least important, and each VIP needs a ranking. The top item gets a 1 and the second gets a 2 and so on.
- Here is some helpful logic to get you through this. If you could only do one of these at a time, which one would you choose first? Which one would you choose next? And so on.
- Next, have the team write in their rankings in the left column. Each VIP needs a ranking next to it from each team member.
- Finally, add up the collective rankings of the team for each VIP and see how they are weighted. The sum total of the rankings represents the collective wisdom of the team. Since we are giving our first choice a ranking of 1, the lowest sum is the top priority of the team; conversely, the highest sum is the lowest collectively ranked VIP.
- In case of a tie, you could repeat the process between the tied items. This will sort it out.

DISCUSSION

As a team, talk about your rankings and rationale. Did the list sort itself out? Is there conflict about what is or should be the priority? This dialogue is important as a team. What VIP should lead the way? Which one is dependent on another on the list? Often, there are dependencies, meaning one cannot begin before another is underway or accomplished.

DECISIONS

You must eventually decide which VIPs are going to get your energy and effort in the coming season. Remember, these are cross-ministry work groups that are formed to release the gospel potential of your church. We are at the crux of church leadership and ChurchOS. We are at the heart of shooting smart bullets (not silver bullets) and vision-based decision-making. At first, your job was to determine what *could* be done. You then narrowed that down to what *should* be done. Now you have to declare what *must* be done. Here are some clarifying thoughts that might help.

- Ask yourself these questions: What will create momentum and prepare us to double our kingdom impact? What must be true to double our kingdom impact?
- Limit yourself to one to three VIPs. We've written a bit about the less-is-more principle of ChurchOS. This is definitely true here. You are about to inject all kinds of new effort on behalf of vision into your church; however, you are also about to task people who are likely already near capacity. We found from experience, one or two VIPs at a time is a good place to begin.
- If you limit yourself as we recommend, you will immediately realize what is not going to receive any new effort now. We've seen this become a stumbling block to some. Remember, we are lining up the initial work. When you complete one VIP, you should be ready to knock out another one—after a little discovery work.

- You don't need to abandon any current goals or efforts unless they are directly related to a VIP and need to be included. You will still be doing church each week and marching through your current calendar. You will now be blending in a new effort.

Many churches operate under a free-market system. There was a time when this was very attractive. Adding more and more ministries or initiatives was seen as a way to increase impact. But we found over time more work only leads to greater costs and fewer returns. In a free-market setting, everyone is free to do what they like. We need to be careful with our freedom. The apostle Paul wisely addressed the issue of Christian freedom in 1 Corinthians 10:23: "'I have the right to do anything,' you say—but not everything is beneficial. 'I have the right to do anything'—but not everything is constructive"(NIV).

You are not looking for what you *can* do but what you *must* do. Focus on what is beneficial and constructive, and you'll see a pattern emerge between those initiatives that are pet projects, a way for a certain person to gain attention, and true, God-directed ministries that activate the Great Commission.

BUILDING A VIP TEAM

Here is a simple format for building a great cross-ministry VIP team. It's easy and at the same time there is so much opportunity in building one of these projects. We use a four-box design to start with, and we will walk you through what to do in each box. The format is not as important as the topics represented in each box. Again, you can use a whiteboard, a piece of paper, or an easel pad.

OBJECTIVE
The objective of the VIP is the purpose for which it was formed. It is a clear, concise sentence or two that explains how everyone will see if

the VIP is accomplished. Good objective statements use verbs and, if possible, contain measurable, objectifying outcomes.

Let's use small group ministry as an example VIP. Your team has decided that an overhaul of your small group ministry should be a strategic focus in the coming season. This conviction was born from the discovery that Piston 2 (Life-Changing Relationships) was seriously misfiring. It is

VIP	
Objective	**Deliverables**
Team - Leader: - Members:	**Next Steps**

glowing red on the Great Commission Engine because you don't have a unified strategy, a leadership development plan, a way to connect the ONE, or enough small groups to satisfy the demand.

The following would be a strong objective statement for this VIP:

> The objective is to unify our small group strategy and double our church's participation in small groups in the next twelve months.

DELIVERABLES

A VIP's deliverables are the subjects or items that must be included for this VIP to be accomplished. They define the scope of the project and are typically discovered over time as the VIP team undertakes the work.

Here are some example VIP deliverables:

- Research from other churches
- A unified written description of a small group model
- A connection plan for our ONE
- A communication plan

- A set of ongoing metrics for healthy small group ministry
- Reporting mechanisms and plan
- Others TBD

TEAM

VIP teams hold incredible potential for your church. They are the breeding ground of future leaders. They are opportunities to bring someone inside your church leadership team. You can leverage volunteers and experts in various arenas and create incredible ownership.

Here are some thoughts about filling the team roles that might be helpful:

- VIP team leader
  - Quarterback of the team
  - Keep the team organized
  - Creates accountability
  - Good at executing a plan
  - May or may not have experience in the VIP subject. It's more important the leader drive the VIP toward its objective.
- VIP team members (four to eight, based on the work necessary to accomplish the VIP)
  - Subject matter experience
  - Key volunteer / ministry stakeholder
  - New or young leaders
  - Passion to see your church grow
  - Deep knowledge of your church

NEXT STEPS

Never finish building a VIP before laying out some concrete next steps *with* dates! We've seen teams not do this for some reason. It's a recipe for a lack of follow-through if you don't.

Here's an example of some initial steps with dates:

- Review VIP with elders by [date].
- Recruit new team member involvement by [date].
- Hold initial VIP team meeting on [date].
- Complete research by [date].
- Complete phase one by [date].
- Our VIP team next steps are [create a list].

CREATE AN IMMEDIATE ACTION LIST

You inevitably will have lots of action items at this point that aren't fitting within a particular VIP. You have done a great job of going through diligent and thorough discovery and addressing key design elements for your church, and now you have a list of thoughts on which you can take action. Don't end this phase of your work before listing some immediate action items with owners and due dates.

Immediate action items are not VIPs. Earlier we mentioned the idea of painting the lobby as a to-do and overhauling the facility as a VIP. During your sessions, your team may determine your interiors are not suited for a church that reaches and connects with the ONE. If that's the case, put "paint the lobby" on the to-do list, assign an owner, and if it's not a part of an emerging VIP, give the owner a deadline for completion.

CREATE A LIST OF THINGS TO STOP DOING

We have dedicated serious time to cover the topic of resource priorities. Remember, church leadership is a zero-sum environment. There is no innocent yes, which means you may need to have a serious conversation with your team about what can go on hold, what can slow down, and what can be moved to a back burner.

We've seen leaders and teams really trip up on this idea. Church leaders just aren't very good at ending things and trimming back ministry, but at times it must be done. Why? So you can devote resources to what's most important. Good may not be best. Possible may not be expedient. We pray your conviction is growing and, if needed, you can make a list of things to stop doing, with a plan for each. If needed, you can review the chart you created for the ministry buffet to see what options are rising to the surface.

Communication will be required if you are going to follow through on your list of things to stop doing. Always lead with *why* when it comes to communicating about these decisions. Speak with love *and* conviction. Move the decision from the realm of opinion to objectified decision-making about your double kingdom vision and about reaching the ONE. The best way to do this is through the power of story, life transformation, and testimonies. God will reward your courage!

ESTABLISH AN ACTIVATOR

One of your last organize steps is to establish an internal point person who creates accountability and ownership for ChurchOS and ongoing Intentional Growth Planning. We call this role the *activator*, and their primary job is to see that the teams are accomplishing their VIPs, blending your today effort with your tomorrow effort, and growing in the disciplines of ChurchOS and IGP. Here are a few thoughts for selecting your activator:

- Deep love for Christ, the ONE, and your church
- Exemplifies what it means to be fully committed
- Must carry the weight of senior leadership or be fully endorsed
- Naturally appreciates discipline and accountability
- Willing to continue the learning about IGP and ChurchOS
- Strategically intuitive but appreciates details and accomplishing goals

Here is some advice on being an activator from David Robbins, the people development leader at The Church at Battlecreek, Tulsa, Oklahoma: "The activator must be a person who has the focus and courage to stick with it. It takes someone saying, "Whoa! We said this is our ONE. Why are we doing this?"

David is not the first activator from his church. He came into the role after the church did a refresh with us at Intentional Churches. "In our first lap, we honestly missed a lot," he said. "We did a lot of Vision Initiative Projects on teams. We advanced some things and created a dashboard, but we missed the whole concept of Great Commission Engine, and it didn't get driven through the organization. We kind of stalled."

For a while, VIP teams became an ugly word around David's church. Staff (who were already busy) would have to meet twice monthly on another project. He explained, "It seemed like a lot of activity, but it wasn't tied to the overall vision." But David, who was interested and invested in the process, wanted to become a coach. David went to the coaches training and stepped behind the curtain of Intentional Churches. He said, "I realized everything we had missed the first time around and the importance of the activator championing the process." David became passionate about refreshing the church's experience and committed to gaining a better understanding the Great Commission Engine. "We have kept perspective of the why behind the what. The VIPs we are now doing are huge. They are twelve-month VIPs and going well," he shared.

One thing David did to advance the concept of the Great Commission Engine was to adhere to the values but use language the church was already familiar with. One staff member said he needed a lexicon to help him understand what was going on, so David wrote one. He took the existing external values of the church and placed them within the language of the Great Commission Engine. He explained, "For example, Piston 1 is called the Catalytic Weekend Experience. So a great weekend worship experience is about site-to-street-to-seat.

In our existing language and values, it is 'the presence of God changes everything.' If we are excelling at a great weekend experience, we are going to move our ONE along his discipling journey. Piston 2 is Life-Changing Relationships or rich community. At our church, we say 'life is better together.' Piston 3 (Surrendered Living) means 'helping people find their purpose in the church and the world and you can never out-give God.'"

An assigned activator is very important, especially in terms of her or his commitment to living in the tension between today and tomorrow. Like David Robbins, the activator must have the creativity and tenacity to walk alongside church staff and leaders as they gain an understanding of the concepts and grow in the disciplines needed to accomplish the vision of double kingdom impact.

Intentional Churches know how to discern the next season's work, clarify it, and organize the personnel and action to get it done. With zero-sum thinking in mind, they know how to stop doing what is less important so they can conserve resources for what is most important. They create internal accountability and know when the work is truly finished and effectively removing barriers to Great Commission activation.

BACK TO THE BATTLE

You have paused as a team and taken the time to discover the truth of today's battle. You have designed the key elements of your battle plan (your ONE, the Engagement Pathway, and your five-year vision for double kingdom impact). In this chapter you have organized yourself and determined what work must be done in the next season (your VIPs). Now it's time to return to the battlefield and blend your efforts together. You must put your energy into today's work. At the same time, you must be focused on tomorrow and releasing your gospel potential. ChurchOS and Intentional Growth Planning must become your operating system and way of life.

FACELIFT, FUNERAL, OR FUEL IT?

FIRST BAPTIST CHURCH—ORLANDO, FLORIDA

Matthew Robinson

One of our VIP teams was to conduct a ministry and activity audit based on looking at our ONE and the Great Commission Engine. This team was to make recommendations but not decisions. This team had to have honest, difficult conversations about why we were still doing some things. We decided that when it came to ministry decisions, we should either invest in it, kill it, or transition it to something else. We called the VIP team Facelift, Funeral, or Fuel It. Looking at all our ministries through the lens of the Great Commission Engine resulted in greater clarity, and we began to answer the questions, What piston does this ministry program go into? Where is it in terms of priority to our mission and vision to grow the church?

The broadcast ministry was one of those we recommended having a funeral for, and it was approved by leadership. We spent several thousand dollars to televise our Sunday morning services, but we realized our ONE was not watching the broadcasts.

By saying no to this mode of ministry, we were able to say yes to improving our Discover Experience, which costs about $67 per person to do. The Discover Experience came from another VIP team that focused on the Engagement Pathway. The Discover Experience features an incredible meal, a free backpack, and a chance to hear from our lead pastor and others while exploring what it looks like to connect and belong on this journey with God and the church.

Sometimes, without realizing it, our strategy was to drain resources and create frustration. Now I ask my teams, "What is the nondisclosed strategy?" because there is one. Everyone is operating on some set of principles or decision-making filters, because we are all making decisions all day long. When it is intentional and aligned, there can be maximum impact.

A FRIEND-TO-FRIEND VIP TEAM

WEST SIDE CHRISTIAN CHURCH—SPRINGFIELD, ILLINOIS

Melissa Sandel

During every round of Intentional Growth Planning, we have different VIP teams emerge, but one that is pretty consistent for us is a Friend-to-Friend VIP team. This has notched up our intentionality, language, and rhythms. We put all of our eggs in the friend-to-friend basket by equipping our people with the right tools. At the start of every worship series, we give cards to people to give to their friends. We do a lot of social media, again encouraging friends to invite friends.

We do a friend-to-friend series every season, designed for someone who is unchurched or de-churched who may have a felt need. Whether they believe in Jesus or not, they know they need help. We've also used some guest speakers who have high appeal to people who are unchurched. The biggest appeal was Darryl Strawberry. He is super genuine and his name drew a lot of people. He was also very gracious afterward.

Before using VIP Teams, our planning was in specific silos. While there is value to the individual ministry plan (you have to have some silos for ministry excellence), cross-functional teams allow us to go farther faster. We are a one-hundred-year-old church that is still writing new chapters to our story!

For more stories and case studies, please visit
www.intentionalchurches.com.

ACTIVATE

The Intentional Growth Planning core process of ChurchOS includes four phases: discover, design, organize, and activate. You have ascended above the battlefield to discern the truth of today's battle. You have designed the key elements of your battle plan. You have taken time to organize your team around key Vision Initiative Projects, and now it's time to get to work. Activating the Great Commission takes discipline and routines that allow you to remain focused on today's tasks while also preparing for tomorrow's battles. If you want to double your kingdom impact, you must learn the disciplines of activation.

Intentional Growth Planning™ (IGP)

Applying the ChurchOS
Living Toolbox™

1 DISCOVER

2 DESIGN

YOUR CHURCH
Great Commission Engine™
& Double Vision

ACTIVATE
4

ORGANIZE
3

TEN

GO AND GROW: RELEASE THE GOSPEL POTENTIAL OF YOUR CHURCH

Glory to him in the church and in Christ Jesus through
all generations forever and ever! Amen.

EPHESIANS 3:21

Earlier we mentioned Einstein's unified theory of relativity and its impact. The application of this theory has led to the development of innovations too numerous to list, and one of the most important was the harnessing of nuclear power. This led to both the benefit of nuclear energy and the devastation of nuclear weapons.

You may have read about the atomic bombs nicknamed Little Boy and Fat Man that were used to end World War II. These bombs exploded with incredible force. Together they released the equivalent of 72 million pounds of TNT![1] What an amazing display of power. But there's an interesting fact in both cases: only a portion of the available potential energy in each bomb was actually used. The reactions that took place expended only a fraction of the nuclear fuel but still produced power on a scale that had never been seen before. Einstein's unified theory had helped tap into something incredible.

Now, imagine the force for eternal good contained in your church. Imagine the infinite potential through the power of the gospel to change lives and make eternal impact in the name of Jesus. The question at hand is how are you going to release this potential season after season? Again and again? While the atomic bombs of August 1945 were meant to curtail war, your church's potential is meant to make an eternal impact yet to be seen. ChurchOS will help you tap into that potential.

It's time to activate the Great Commission and release the gospel potential of your church. If you've been following along, we believe the local church is God's miracle strategy. We are also in partnership with him, as were Paul and Apollos, planting and watering, expecting him to bring the increase. The fact that God has invited us to partner in leading his church, the bride of Christ, is both humbling and challenging.

We are going to show you how to activate the Great Commission and ensure progress toward your five-year double kingdom impact vision. But before we do, we need to review the basics about ChurchOS.

Many books have been written about church growth. What's new about ChurchOS is the way the growth fundamentals are addressed through strategic conversations and tools. These work together to produce Great Commission activation and a growing outcome. One piece is not more important than another, and together they have greater impact than separately. No matter how tempted you are to use only one part, it's the whole that matters—the system.

Let's briefly review the fundamentals of the system.

SIX DOMAINS OF CHURCH: This represents the sum total of church leadership. You must have a plan for each of these areas, and ChurchOS, in its entirety, is made to address each of them. You are getting the fundamentals in this book. (See the graphic on page 22.)

INTENTIONAL GROWTH PLANNING (IGP): This is the core, cyclical process of

ChurchOS that involves the four phases of discovery, design, organize, and activate. It is built to be used at the highest level of leadership and throughout your ministry to assess your spiritual battlefield. (See the graphic on page 27.)

THE LIVING TOOLBOX: This is the ever-growing suite of strategic conversations and tools used to run ChurchOS and Intentional Growth Planning. You have learned the base set of those tools in this book. One of the keys to ChurchOS is having the right strategic conversations at the right time and in the right sequence. (See the graphic on page 26.)

THE GREAT COMMISSION ENGINE (GCE): This is the tool that lays the biblical foundation of ChurchOS. It's an analogy used to simplify strategy and to study how to power Great Commission activation in every church. (See the graphic on page 50.)

THE ONE: The system revolves around the lost, namely, reaching them for Christ, initiating them, and teaching them to obey his commandments. Disciples who make disciples are focused on Christ's mission of seeking and saving the lost as well as focused on obedience. A focus on evangelism and obedience grows everyone.

These fundamentals come together to create ChurchOS. This is important to understand because Great Commission activation and double kingdom impact requires you to know how these parts work together. If you were to remove any layer, the system would be incomplete and would break down.

Now, let's put ChurchOS in motion. Let's activate!

THE ACTIVATOR ROLE

First things first, the activator role is vital to installing and running ChurchOS. We discussed this in the last chapter. A point person on your team needs to own these tools (repeatable, strategic, biblically based conversations) as well as the implementation and proliferation of the system. If you are the ChurchOS activator at your church, this chapter is especially for you, but every leader and team member should read it.

ACTIVATION DASHBOARD OVERVIEW

The primary activation tool you are going to use is a compilation of the ChurchOS elements you have already developed. We call it the *Activation Dashboard*, and you will use it to navigate toward your vision of double kingdom impact.

You've probably taken a road trip. We have. California is a common destination for us. It's about a four-hour drive from our homes in Las Vegas to the beach and other popular spots there. These trips require planning and preparation. There is scheduling, packing, and filling the car up with gas. You walk around the car and take an honest assessment of how things look. You enter the destination into a GPS or an app on your phone and off you go. As you drive, you monitor your speed, fuel, and estimated time of arrival. The ride is filled with visions and anticipations of what's to come, but without focus and determination, you could end up delayed or, worse, at the wrong destination.

Now, you are ready to begin the ChurchOS journey. You've walked around your ministry and taken an honest assessment of today's realities and tomorrow's challenges. You've made a plan and designed certain key elements of your ministry to ensure you are on the right road. You have a map and have programmed the GPS to point you toward your five-year vision of double impact. You've fueled up with the power of prayer and the Holy Spirit, and now it's time to embark. Before doing so, however, you must put together a dashboard to stay in front of you on this journey. This dashboard must contain high-level information to help you steer your church in the right direction.

The ChurchOS Activation Dashboard is purposeful but simple. It reduces the system to a few key items to monitor. If you have carefully walked through the phases of Intentional Growth Planning to this point (discovery, design, and organize), you can be sure this is the right tool. Nothing more is necessary to embark and manage what's next. This is the rollout of your hard work and effort to this point.

ChurchOS Activation Dashboard™

Activators	Activation Measurements			VIPs	
Great Commission Engine™ (GCE)	Measurable	1 YR	5 YR	Title & Leader	Status
				Leader:	Status R/Y/G
				Leader:	Status R/Y/G
Status R/Y/G				Leader:	Status R/Y/G

Don't let the image of the Activation Dashboard intimidate you. It may look daunting and complicated, but it's really simple and profound. It is intuitive if you're familiar with the aspects we just covered and involves only three panels. Each panel contains a high-level element of ChurchOS. When you put them together, you get the dashboard that will guide you. Practically speaking, think of it as three sheets of easel paper

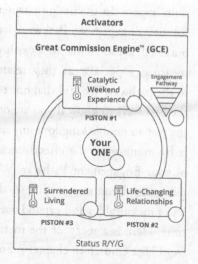

Activators

Great Commission Engine™ (GCE)

Catalytic Weekend Experience

Engagement Pathway

PISTON #1

Your ONE

Surrendered Living

PISTON #3

Life-Changing Relationships

PISTON #2

Status R/Y/G

arranged next to each other on a wall or three sheets of paper making up a single report.

Let's look at each panel.

PANEL #1: VISION ACTIVATORS: THE GREAT COMMISSION ENGINE AND RATINGS

At the highest level, these five things will activate the Great Commission and drive you toward double kingdom impact. Earlier in the book you walked through the biblical background of the GCE and then rated the status of each component in your church. We also had you rate the GCE a second time after you developed the key design elements of the ONE, the Engagement Pathway, and double vision. If one of the components of the GCE is weak, you are losing Great Commission activation horsepower. At the same time, it is hard to keep all of them equally strong simultaneously. Remember, your GCE is under constant strain as you strive for double kingdom impact with a rolling five-year vision.

PANEL #2: VISION ACTIVATION MEASUREMENTS

The center panel contains the measurements of double kingdom impact. In the design chapter for the Engagement Pathway, we outlined some items to possibly measure, especially as they relate to the pathway. We said that one of the best ways to know if you are on the way to double kingdom impact is by monitoring the effectiveness of your Engagement Pathway. We recommend you start with a small set of measurables and expand over

Activation Measurements		
Measurable	1 YR	5 YR

time. Here is a recap of the metrics we laid out from our example from First Church in chapter 7. Start with a similar list or even fewer. Remember, less is better at first!

SAMPLE ENGAGEMENT PATHWAY MEASURABLES

Engagement Pathway	Measurable	Goal
Weekend Worship Service	Average Weekend Attendance (AWA)	Grow by 15% yearly
Baby Steps	Baby steps taken	100% of AWA (annually)
First Step Class	Attendance	20% of AWA (annually)
	Completion	100%
	Salvations	32%–50% of attendance
Conversion / Baptism	Baptisms	20% of AWA (annually)
Second Step Class	Attendance	20% of AWA (annually)
	Group starts	100% of class
	Serve starts	100% of class
	Giving starts	100% of class
Small Groups	Group members	80% of AWA
	Expected # of groups	Group membership/10
Second Step Class	Attendance	100% of AWA (annually)
	Group starts	100% of class attendance
	Serve starts	100% of class attendance
	Giving starts	100% of class attendance
Small Groups	Group members	80% of AWA
	# of Groups	Group membership/10
	Leaders	100% of # of groups
	Apprentice leaders	100% of # of groups
Serve / Give / Share	Servants	40%+ of AWA
Core	Owners	25% of AWA

When you're beginning, keep the layout of your vision activation measurements simple. We recommend you limit both the number of measurables and your goals. At first, your Activation Dashboard can simply have your five-year double kingdom impact goals (these will be inspiring) along with realistic one-year goals. As you grow into ChurchOS, you can expand the number of things you are measuring, and the intervals can become more granular as well.

PANEL #3: VISION INITIATIVE PROJECTS (VIPS)

In the previous chapter, we talked about discerning the next season's work as a team and showed you how to organize cross-ministry work groups. Again, if you've spent ample time in discovery and refreshing your designs, the VIPs often come into view and their priorities are natural and logical. The underlying belief is that if you work your projects to completion, your church will advance, barriers will be removed, and the Great Commission will be activated, which releases the gospel

VIPs	
Title & Leader	Status
Leader:	Status R/Y/G
Leader:	Status R/Y/G
Leader:	Status R/Y/G

potential of your church and allows your double kingdom impact to flow. Once these projects are completed, you will renew your plan and add more projects. Your dashboard includes VIPs because cross-ministry projects and work groups will become a way of life for you and your teams. They are integral to ChurchOS and to advancing the gospel.

HOW TO RATE VIPS

We covered our red-yellow-green rating system in chapter 2. You implemented the system for the Great Commission Engine, but we need to explain how to use it to rate VIPs. We have three ideas in mind to use in rating your VIPs:

- Is the VIP progressing according to plan?
- Is the VIP drifting in its purpose?
- Is the VIP fully implemented?

Great Commission activation comes down to using your Activation Dashboard to monitor the status of today's Great Commission activities, along with the work it will take to release the gospel potential of your church. The center panel will help you monitor your progress. By using it regularly, you will drive the right strategic conversations at the right time and in the right sequence.

USING THE ACTIVATION DASHBOARD

We're about to get very practical. ChurchOS is going to come down to the rhythms and routines you develop. It's in these that you will align your team and create unparalleled focus on the Great Commission that leads to activation and double kingdom impact.

The following are the steps to implementing the Activation Dashboard.

STEP 1: DRAW OR DOWNLOAD A COPY OF THE GREAT COMMISSION ENGINE

You are going to make periodic reviews of the GCE routine for your team. We've seen teams print out a large version on foam board so they can hang it on a wall, or they print them on easel-sized sheets. You can also leave the Activation Dashboard in its digital form and use it that way after you download it.

STEP 2: ASSIGN OWNERSHIP OF YOUR VISION ACTIVATION MEASUREMENTS

This panel contains your agreed-upon measurements with updated goals and real measurements. Assign this to a team member to build and keep updated. Some teams have used Google Docs, Excel spreadsheets, and other software to build and maintain the center panel. It may take a bit of work if you do not monitor these things, but it will pay off to make the effort. Someone with skills in this area will find this job very rewarding!

STEP 3: DRAW OR DOWNLOAD A COPY OF YOUR VIPS STATUS PANEL

The third panel will help create accountability for the execution of your VIPs. Some teams have re-created the full three-panel design and hung it on a wall, some have shared the documents via the cloud, and some have printed it out as a simple report on standard paper. You need to find an approach that will work for your team.

STEP 4: ESTABLISH YOUR ACTIVATION DASHBOARD REVIEW PROCESS

This is where ChurchOS implementation requires some customization. When, how, and where you implement the review of the dashboard is up to you and needs to dovetail with your current meetings and rhythms. In some cases, you will need to establish new meetings and routines in order to embed this into your leadership. Some teams have made the review process part of their staff meetings, elder meetings, or lead team meetings.

To help you, in the next section we are going to outline the routines and rhythms of ChurchOS. The rewards of activation and double kingdom impact require discipline, but on the other side of discipline is eternal impact and great glory for God. Again, if you are the activator for your church, it will be your job to map out this plan.

CHURCHOS RHYTHM GUIDELINES

Here is a grid to help you establish your routines for reviewing your Activation Dashboard and fully implementing ChurchOS. Use this to map out what element will be covered in what meeting, how often, and by whom.

Using the grid and a calendar, you can lay out your meeting schedule and predetermine what component of ChurchOS makes the agenda. Here are some optional ways to flow the components into your meetings based on frequency:

CHURCHOS RHYTHM GUIDELINES

ChurchOS Component	Frequency
Vision Activators / Great Commission Engine	Quarterly
Today's VIP Status	At least monthly
Vision Activation Measurements Review	3–6 months
Vision Activation Measurements Updated	Weekly
Four Helpful Lists	As needed (often!)
Your ONE Design	1–3 years
Engagement Pathway Design	Ongoing
Five-Year Double Kingdom Impact Vision Design	1–2 years
Adding New VIPs / Immediate Action	Ongoing
Team-Wide Master IGP / ChurchOS Renewal	12–18 months
ChurchOS Activation Assessment	12–18 months

WEEKLY

- Four Helpful Lists is used in the meeting as often as needed.
- Immediate action lists are discussed, reviewed, and updated.
- Optional: one VIP could be reviewed each week.
- Optional: one component of the Great Commission Engine is reviewed and the status updated, with components rotated weekly.
- Vision measurements are updated and ready for review.

MONTHLY

- VIPs are reviewed for progress, and the status of each is updated.
- Engagement Pathway is reviewed for performance.

QUARTERLY

- Vision measurements are updated and reviewed.
- Every component of the Great Commission Engine is reviewed and updated.

ANNUALLY

- Master IGP renewed through the complete cycle of discovery, design, and organize phases.
- The definition of your ONE is reviewed completely and updated as needed.
- Five-year double kingdom impact is reviewed and updated as needed.

AS NEEDED

- VIPs completed with new VIPs created.
- Four Helpful Lists used as primary discovery tool.

WARNING! You probably have a question or two about these guidelines. Maybe the fact that measurements are only reviewed quarterly to biannually popped up. There's a reason for this, and it comes with the following warning. We believe a contributor to silver-bullet thinking and, at times, impetuous leadership is the chance that we fixate on the numbers or measurements. This leads to quick decisions that are not based in discovery or proper Great Commission design and can be very costly, as we outlined earlier in this book. A fixation on numbers can be destructive and counterproductive. We rank it as one of the top issues in church leadership and a bad habit that needs to be broken or, at the least, reinvented.

Here are a few things to remember about measurements. They ebb and flow from week to week. Trends over time matter more. Measurements are actually the results or outcomes of a well-executed plan to double your kingdom impact. They are downline of the Great Commission Engine and indicative of your direction toward a destination, not the destination itself. As we all know, measurements alone don't tell the real story. They can give both a false sense of doom and security, especially if you look at them too often. What's more important is closely monitoring what drives the outcomes you want and what strategic work is in front of you right now that, if you do it, will release your gospel potential.

Your rhythms and routines of ChurchOS will determine your success. They will drive the right strategic conversations at the right time and in the right sequence. As you are diagnosing, reviewing, and learning together, great questions will become your best friends.

ASKING GREAT QUESTIONS

Einstein supposedly said, "If I had an hour to solve a problem and my life depended on the solution, I would spend the first fifty-five minutes determining the proper questions to ask."

Good leaders ask questions rather than make statements. Asking questions is a powerful skill that represents humility, selflessness, and care. You have to get outside yourself and leverage your intuition to ask good, clarifying questions. It's a learned craft that takes practice and repetition. In the book *Multipliers: How the Best Leaders Make Everyone Smarter*, Liz Wiseman wrote, "A bad leader will tell people what to do. A good leader will ask questions and let his or her people figure out the answers. A great leader asks the questions that focus the intelligence of their team on the right problems."[2]

Have you noticed how Jesus leveraged the power of great questions? In fact, he used questions better than any teacher. You might be surprised his primary go-to method for teaching was asking questions. He does this more than 175 times in the Gospels. At very critical times, instead of giving an answer, he asked a question.

Here are a few examples. Just reading them can prompt the Holy Spirit's leading. Which of the following questions resonates with your soul today?

- "Do you love me?" (John 21:15–17)
- "Who do you say I am?" (Matt. 16:15)
- "What do you want?" (John 1:38)
- "Why do you have such evil thoughts in your hearts?" (Matt. 9:4)

- "Can all your worries add a single moment to your life?" (Matt. 6:27)
- "Why do you keep calling me 'Lord, Lord!' when you don't do what I say?" (Luke 6:46)
- "Why are you afraid?" (Mark 4:40)
- "Where is your faith?" (Luke 8:25)
- "Why did you doubt me?" (Matt. 14:31)
- "What is all this arguing about?" (Mark 9:16)
- "Do you understand what I was doing?" (John 13:12)
- "When I sent you out to preach the Good News and you did not have money, a traveler's bag, or an extra pair of sandals, did you need anything?" (Luke 22:35)
- "Die for me?" (John 13:38)
- "Have I been with you all this time . . . and yet you still don't know who I am?" (John 14:9)
- "Is this your own question, or did others tell you about me?" (John 18:34)

Maybe the most effective tool you have is a good question. Chances are far greater that if you want answers and are praying for God to speak to you and your team, he'll speak to you in the form of a question instead of an answer.

We believe in the discipline, art, and effort to ask questions and not make statements as you lead your church. Devote yourself to the craft and it will pay dividends.

One of the benefits of ChurchOS is that some of the questions you need to be asking come prepackaged for you. But there is no way to give you every question you need to ask your team. You must develop your own over time. For Intentional Churches, the following is a short list of the elements of some great questions.

- Designed to drive insight and self-discovery
- Never asked passive-aggressively

- Never about an off-topic agenda
- Selfless in nature
- Patient for the answer to come
- Based on the ChurchOS foundations

You've probably noticed we've used questions throughout this book as the primary means to drive insight and decisions. These questions are set against the clarifying framework of the ChurchOS fundamentals. Without this baseline understanding, the questions would be soft and would not drive meaningful outcomes in terms of gospel impact. The two work together: the framework of the system and the questions. The biblical foundations of the Great Commission Engine and the tension of double kingdom impact create an opportunity for great questions.

Here's a list of a few ChurchOS-type questions:

- Will this help us to double our kingdom impact?
- Is this today's priority or tomorrow's?
- What is today's status in terms of a snapshot?
- How does this strategy fit the Great Commission Engine?
- Does this strategy turn a yellow rating into a green rating?
- Is this going to advance us toward our true north?
- Does this create stagnation or spiritual movement?
- What must be true in the coming season for us to meet our goals?
- Does this measurement align with our five-year vision outcomes?
- Is this ministry a cul-de-sac or is it creating squatters?
- What can we put on hold so we can better use our resources in the next season?
- We know what could and should be done eventually, but what must be done now?
- Who owns this? When will it be done?
- What does green mean? yellow? red?
- Where is the fear? What do we hope for?

Get the picture? ChurchOS is about creating an objective biblical standard so critical, clarifying questions can be asked and objective answers can be discerned for your church and the sake of the Great Commission. This has incredible power to cut through silver-bullet thinking and impetuous leadership. It will also create deep ownership because of the process of self-discovery. By implementing and using ChurchOS, you and your team will quickly come to a shared understanding of how to grow your kingdom impact in the right way. Incredible alignment is about to set in.

MONITORING ACTIVATION

ChurchOS ACTIVATION ASSESSMENT (ADVANCED)

We have created an assessment tool to help you with alignment. It will also be your guide as you implement ChurchOS. It's categorically built to give you a point-by-point status report on various components and elements of the ChurchOS system. It is also giving you an overall rating to monitor. We recommend you give the quiz below to several people once they are familiar with the system. Comparing your scores and thoughts will create great leadership conversations. We recommend you take the assessment every twelve to eighteen months or more often. By repeating the cycles of the ChurchOS system and Intentional Growth Planning, you will see improved scores and better and better kingdom results.

We gave you a generic assessment earlier in the book, but now that you are more familiar with ChurchOS, you should take it again. You should better understand most of the benchmarks and be able to rate your implementation. We are convinced about these benchmarks because we've seen simple improvements in just one area lead to tremendous momentum. These twenty-one benchmarks are at the heart of ChurchOS. They will deliver sustained Great Commission activation through diligent implementation and evaluation.

Before you begin, remember our evaluation standards and scoring system from chapter 2. You are putting the system into practice by judging your church against the big ideas of sustained Great Commission activation and double kingdom impact.

Hint: If you use this assessment methodology with those big ideas in mind, you should never get a perfect score, because double vision is an ever-evolving frontier (as you now know). As the horizon shifts, the scores should change, because your dreams are getting bigger and your goals are becoming loftier.

Grade yourself as a team.

Place an X in the box that represents your grade. (R = red, Y = yellow, G = green)

	Question	R (1 point)	Y (3 points)	G (6 points)
1	MISSION: We understand the mission of the local church is the Great Commission and have restated it clearly in our own terms.			
2	VISION: We have a clear five-year vision for the development of our ONE and double impact of our church that is owned by all. It is refreshed every twelve to twenty-four months.			
3	EVALUATION: We evaluate everything we do through the lenses of Great Commission activation, double impact, and reaching our ONE. Our team understands our evaluation standards and methods.			
4	THE LAST 10 PERCENT: We are deeply honest as a team about our church and our relationships. We understand we are only stewards of the Lord's church and thus we can be objective about its plans and strategies.			

5	**THE GREAT COMMISSION ENGINE:** We understand the Great Commission Engine, how to evaluate each of the five components with the ONE and double impact in mind, and we regularly review it to create clarity and alignment.			
6	**PRIORITIES FOR IMPACT:** Our ministry strategies are prioritized and reviewed at least annually and resources allocated accordingly. We limit our ministry buffet and do not let it stifle our resources. We have no sacred cows.			
7	**FOCUS ON OUR ONE:** Our church is built to reach and develop our ONE. Our team understands the personality, driving motivations, and the state of the ONE's life. This a key filter for strategizing and decision-making.			
8	**ENGAGEMENT PATHWAY:** We have a defined pathway that is built to connect our ONE to us, Christ, and one another. The system is built on the baby-step principle and is measured, evaluated, and constantly improved.			
9	**ACTIVATION DASHBOARD:** We have a clearly defined vision activation road map. It includes the Great Commission Engine, vision measurements, and focus points for the next season. It is our heads-up display and is owned and reviewed regularly.			
10	**THE NEXT SEASON'S WORK:** We are clear about the work that must be accomplished in the next season to release the gospel potential of our church. We are constantly organized in cross-ministry work groups to accomplish this work in addition to our day-to-day responsibilities.			

11	**STRUCTURE AND ROLES:** We know who is doing what and when it's being done. We monitor our progress accordingly. Our roles and organization chart make sense, and we know how to measure individual success. We know how to manage the strategic work that intersects with the daily operations of our ministry.			
12	**MEETINGS:** We know how to run great meetings. We know who to include in tomorrow-oriented meetings and today-oriented meetings. The calendar, rhythm, and cadence of our meetings make sense for Great Commission activation. Our meeting agendas make sense.			
13	**COMMON LANGUAGE:** We use consistent language and definitions to create alignment, clarity, and efficiency. This language is owned by pastors, staff, leaders, and volunteers.			
14	**IGP DEPLOYMENT AND TRAINING:** We have Intentional Growth Plans established across our ministries. Each major area of our ministry is using IGP and running ChurchOS.			
15	**ACTIVATION OWNERSHIP:** We have identified a champion (activator) who holds us accountable to Great Commission activation. This champion is trained in IGP and constantly learning about ChurchOS. We have given permission to our activator to challenge and lead us.			

16	SILVER BULLETS: We know how to plug in the latest ministry solutions in a way that doesn't distract us from the biblical fundamentals of ChurchOS. These solutions add to our impact over time. We don't consider them sacred, but we seek to gain Great Commission impact while constantly monitoring them for effectiveness.			
17	GOVERNANCE AND DECISION MAKING: The model for our board, committees, teams, and general decision-making model is fit for today and ready for tomorrow's adjustments. We know how to make decisions effectively with appropriate speed. Responsibility and authority are clear to our team.			
18	GENEROSITY: We know that vision creates ownership, and generosity comes with ownership. We are effective at regularly casting vision, inspiring generosity, and calling for increased financial sacrifice in the light of our Great Commission Double Vision.			
19	LEADERSHIP DEVELOPMENT: We know how to develop leaders at all levels in a way that increases our leadership base and span of care. We can identify this pathway and subsequently identify who is on the pathway and how it is performing. We can clearly identify who is on mission with us.			
20	PRAYER: We have a proactive plan for prayer to release the power of the Holy Spirit. We know that prayer and the Holy Spirit fuel Great Commission activation and evangelistic growth.			

21	MULTIPLYING: We are convicted and praying about multiplying, including sites, church plants, and teaching other churches how to use ChurchOS and IGP to activate the Great Commission and double their kingdom impact.			

Our score in each area is:

Total number of red marks x 1 = _____

Total number of yellow marks x 3 = _____

Total number of green marks x 6 = _____

Our grand total is _____

Here is the key to the assessment. Chart your score.

0	60	120
Red (<22)	Yellow (22–60)	Green (61–120)
(Mark an X below where you scored in the continuum.)		

The scoring is weighted because there is incredible power in the principles beneath these twenty-one benchmarks. If you improve only slightly in one of these areas, it can have great impact in your church. We've seen it!

Many of our churches started close to the red zone, have moved into the yellow, and are already seeing God move in big ways. Yes, we have yellow-zone churches on pace to double in five years. That's the power of the principles of ChurchOS. And green-zone churches have room for improvement, but you would be hard-pressed to find a green-zone church that isn't gaining momentum or growing rapidly through evangelistic effort.

This assessment comes with a warning! Do not fall victim to drawing conclusions too quickly, trying to fix everything with silver-bullet thinking or shortsighted decisions. Those days are over! Use the core process of Intentional Growth Planning to lead your team to the right work for the next season. Remember the disciplines of the four phases: discovery, design, organize, and activate.

WHERE TO START?

Here are some guidelines for installing ChurchOS and beginning the Intentional Church journey. As you might imagine, no two journeys are the same. You will need to map the implementation plan that makes sense for you and your team. The pace of implementation is what probably matters most for the system to take root and have long-term impact.

DIGEST AND USE THE GREAT COMMISSION ENGINE

The system rests on the biblical underpinnings of the Great Commission Engine. All five components matter and work together as a system, but each component has nuance and details worth discussing and understanding as a team. Don't move on to other aspects of ChurchOS until your team is familiar with and in agreement on the Great Commission Engine. Furthermore, the GCE components are a customized application for your church, meaning the way you execute on Piston 1 (Catalytic Weekend Experience) is unique to you. Remember, it's a total experience. It's worth mapping out what this experience includes for you, your church, and your ONE so everyone understands what this means. This language and common understanding will be powerful. One component alone should be discussed until it's understood clearly. Remember to include all of your leadership stakeholders in the conversation. It's important to have your elders, deacons, and board members aligned with the GCE.

TAKE YOUR TIME WITH THE DESIGN TOOLS (YOUR ONE, THE ENGAGEMENT PATHWAY, AND YOUR FIVE-YEAR DOUBLE VISION)

Each of these design components is fundamental to the ChurchOS system. And each of these are potentially weighty topics for a team to consider.

For instance, discerning your ONE will take a lot of prayer, study, discussion, and contemplation. Remember, we recommend that you imbalance your leadership toward the ONE. You need to create a thorough ONE-aware filter and use it! Make sure your team buys into these design elements enough to move toward confident action. By taking action, your team will learn whether you are zeroing in on the right design elements or not.

DON'T BITE OFF MORE THAN YOU CAN HANDLE

We have learned that one or two VIPs at a time is plenty of work to integrate into your existing fifty-two-week effort. You will be tempted to take on more work at first. You will also be tempted to move quickly and skip the steps outlined in the organize phase of Intentional Growth Planning. If your team has walked well through the discovery and design phases, there will be excitement about the work ahead and a sense of urgency. There's great danger in overloading the team and rushing into the work. Walk through the organize phase carefully, and then get to work.

BE PATIENT, BE PATIENT, BE PATIENT

It takes time for this system to develop and for your team to learn to use it until it becomes natural. Time! It's kind of like chess in that it's easy to learn the rules and concepts, but there's a lifetime of learning in the application and mastery of the game. ChurchOS will become second nature for your team after they have cycled through Intentional Growth Planning at least twice. Each cycle provides more insight. The team *then* moves faster. Discernment gains clarity and the outcomes are more poignant. Give yourself at least a year to roll out the system. If you roll it out sooner, great. If it takes longer, don't beat yourself up. You will see reward long before ChurchOS is fully embedded in your church. We promise!

SET REALISTIC EXPECTATIONS

It's important to emotionally prepare yourself for this journey. You are about to embark on something that is going to stir people up. In good and productive ways it's going to fire up some people. In challenging ways it's going to create significant change. You are going to be establishing new routines and questioning old norms. You may be deciding to end some ministries or start new ones. You may be radically changing your church in time as you reach more and more of the ONE from your community. As you do, keep in mind the upside of a church that is clear, focused, and aligned around double kingdom impact. Think about the lives that will be changed for eternity and the ripple effect you will only know about in heaven. Above all else, pray often, listen to the Spirit, and remember the admonition of Joshua to "be strong and courageous!" (Josh. 1:9). It was *not* a recommendation. It was a command!

SHIP SOMETHING

Finally, realize you are going to learn a lot as you go into this process. There is a phrase used by entrepreneurs: "Ship something!" In other words, the way you get a start-up going is to sell something and ship it. The same is true for you. Once you have a critical mass of leaders on board and enough confidence to embark, go! *Do not* wait until everything is perfectly figured out or every member is on board. Time is of the essence, right? Eternity is at stake. Trust us: learning will accelerate as you take action. You can adjust anything you have developed. You can adjust your insights from discovery and design, the way you're organized, and how you activate. Remember, no strategy or tactic is sacred when it comes to Great Commission activation and double kingdom impact.

DEEPENING AND WIDENING

After taking hundreds of churches through Intentional Growth Planning and helping with the adoption of ChurchOS, we can help you understand the journey ahead. Adoption of the system will take time, but you will see Great Commission impact long before you've fully embedded the rhythm and routines. Knowing what's ahead will also help you fight for the victories that are on the other side of your effort but may not yet be evident.

LAPS DRIVE LEVELS

Think of it this way, the more cycles (laps) of Intentional Growth Planning—discovery, design, organize, activate—with the Great Commission Engine and the Six Domains of Church in focus, the deeper your understanding of ChurchOS (levels). We've created five levels of adoption, and every church we work with starts at level 1. How quickly you progress through the levels will be unique to you, and the deeper you can drive your adoption, the more broadly and deeply you will drive Great Commission activation.

Here is a chart we've created to help you understand the adoption sequence. You can use this chart with the ChurchOS Activation Assessment to know where you are, what's next, and how to set your expectations.

Your ChurchOS™ Adoption Journey

Levels			Deeper & Wider	Intentional Growth Planning™ (IGP)
IGP Lap One	1	Experiencing	Complete IGP Lap One Discover, Design, Organize Establish VIP(s) and Immediate Action Kick-off of ChurchOS Rhythm and Routines	Core Process Laps = Deepening Levels
	2	Learning	Regularly Use the Activation Dashboard Working VIPs to True Completion Rhythm and Routines Become Habits	1 DISCOVER 2 DESIGN
	3	Owning	Establish Trained Internal Activator Expand Use of IGP in Ministry Activating GCE / Vision & Celebrating	YOUR CHURCH Great Commission Engine™ & Double Vision
Advanced	4	Living	IGP Used Throughout All Areas Training Team in IGP Best Practices IGP Laps Established Throughout	4 ACTIVATE ORGANIZE 3
	5	Multiplying	Calendar Reflects ChurchOS Discipline Collaborating Internally and Externally Planning to Help Others Use IGP and ChurchOS	

The chart shows you the status of your deepening adoption of the Living Toolbox, Intentional Growth Planning, and ultimately ChurchOS. It's hard to say how long it will take. We've seen churches make great progress in one year, and it's taken others up to four years. Be patient. This is a learning experience that will be worth the effort, and we will be alongside you to help.

The ChurchOS Activation Assessment will be your ongoing tool to help assess the status of the twenty-one key elements of ChurchOS. Inevitably, it's hard to score a green in every element, but only a few greens can create incredible Great Commission activation. It won't be long until you are on your way to double kingdom impact.

Intentional Churches build ministry dashboards to monitor Great Commission activation and double kingdom vision. They review them regularly and don't fixate on the numbers or make swift or short-sighted decisions. They develop patience and don't take on more than they can handle while seeking to constantly improve. They know the victory is God's to bring.

READY TO GO, READY TO GROW

Jim Collins developed a concept called the twenty-mile march and wrote about it in *Great by Choice.* He uses the analogy of a hike across America to describe enterprises that prevail through self-discipline. The march imposes order amid disorder, discipline amid chaos, and consistency amid uncertainty.

> Imagine you're standing with your feet in the Pacific Ocean in San Diego, California, looking inland. You're about to embark on a three-thousand-mile walk, from San Diego to the tip of Maine. On the first day, you march 20 miles, making it out of town. On the second day, you march 20 miles. And again, on the third day, you march 20 miles, heading into the heat of the desert. It's hot,

more than a hundred degrees, and you want to rest in the cool of your tent. But you don't. You get up and you march 20 miles. You keep the pace, 20 miles a day.

Then the weather cools, and you're in comfortable conditions with the wind at your back, and you could go much farther. But you hold back, modulating your effort. You stick with your 20 miles. . . . You sustain your pace, marching 20 miles. And eventually, you get to Maine.

Now, imagine another person who starts out with you on the same day in San Diego. He gets all excited by the journey and logs 40 miles the first day. Exhausted from his first gigantic day, he wakes up to hundred-degree temperatures. He decides to hang out until the weather cools, thinking, "I'll make it up when conditions improve." He maintains this pattern—big days with good conditions, whining and waiting in his tent on bad days—as he moves across the western United States. . . . By the time he enters Kansas City, you, with your relentless 20-mile march, have already reached the tip of Maine. You win, by a huge margin.[3]

Which of the two hikers reflects you and your church? Churches are full of disorder, chaos, and uncertainty. You need a repeatable operating system that helps you establish your twenty-mile march. We have laid out the sequence in this book. It's contained in the Intentional Growth Planning process: discovery, design, organize, and activate. If you'll use it—along with the Six Domains of Church, the Great Commission Engine, and the ONE in front of you—your church will advance. If you install this as your ChurchOS, you will look back and be amazed at how far you've gone, not by your power but by his.

Are you ready? Are you ready to see double kingdom impact in your church? Are you ready to lay down the silver bullets and start firing smart ones? Are you ready to plant and water and watch him bring the increase?

We can give you the tools. We can provide the training. We

can even give you the support and inspiration of hundreds of stories like the ones in this book. Now, it's up to you to activate the Great Commission and release the gospel potential in your life and in your church.

The story of Gideon is well known. A man who was transformed from fearful and anxious into a great military leader. What made the difference? It wasn't anything within him that changed. God always knew his potential, but one night God told him to go down to an enemy camp and listen as two men discussed a dream (Judg. 7:13–14). That dream was all about the potential they knew was inside Gideon the whole time. And now he knew. He was ready to go into battle!

You may be looking over your battlefield right now and wondering if you're the right person for the job. We want you to know that you are! All it takes is conviction and submission (100 percent) to God's vision and plan. He knows your potential and the potential of your church. He placed you where you need to be. Now it's up to you to join him at his invitation to partner in leading his church. He is with you and will bring the victory.

If you're ready to go, then you're ready to grow.

BOLDLY GO

CROSSROADS CHURCH—CORONA, CALIFORNIA

Galen Thomas

There is nothing magical or mystical about doubling impact, just as there is nothing magical about planning five years out. But when you combine the two—doubling in five years—suddenly nothing you are doing today will work. The brilliance of this is that it forces you to think differently. Incremental tweaking does not get you where you need to go.

Our vision is to Boldly Go to the next generation, and it was and is a big, hairy, audacious goal. We want to reach and keep 13,500 young people, ages two to twenty-nine, within a twenty-mile radius by 2023. It's a one-fund effort that is evangelism focused. Instead of doubling in five years, it is essentially tripling in six. It's been a lot of fun and different thinking for us.

When you are thinking about reaching two-year-olds to twenty-nine-year-olds, some of those people can drive themselves and many can't! So we must *go* to them. One of our strategies is working with our local public schools. One of those partner schools is a middle school that is very under-resourced. They have a girls' and a boys' basketball team that share old uniforms, actually soccer uniforms. Because they only have one basketball court, the girls play first, and when they are done, they take off the jerseys and give them to the boys to play their game. When we heard about that, our church bought uniforms for each team, making a big difference for the kids.

Another strategy to reach the next generation is to refresh and upgrade our online campus. Our online campus has grown by 300 percent—approaching 2,000 people online. We desire to provide a better online experience with hosts and chat. We are also starting Watch Parties, training people to be facilitators and hosts in their homes. These are for people who won't go to church but will go to another person's home and watch church. They are blowing up with ten to twenty people in the same room watching church, discussing it, then eating and watching football afterward.

TEXT "MY FIRST STEP"

CHURCH ON RUSH CREEK—ARLINGTON, TEXAS

Jeff Kirkpatrick

Want to get involved at Rush Creek? Have questions about your faith? Don't know where to start? The First Step Experience is for you! It's a four-week journey full of fun, friends, and coffee. Simply text "my first step" to learn more and get registered. What's included in the four-week journey?

Who Am I in God's Story? *The first Sunday of each month.*

Who Am I As a Christ Follower? *The second Sunday of each month.*

Who Am I As a Partner? (Part 1) *The third Sunday of each month.*

Who Am I As a Partner? (Part 2) *The fourth Sunday of each month.*

You can jump in at any point during the four weeks, and it doesn't matter what question you have. The answer is found at First Step Experience.

PICKING UP THE BATON AND GOING ALL IN!

THE OAKS CHURCH—RED OAK, TEXAS

Hunter Wilson

One of the things I appreciate at The Oaks is that leaders are always looking to hand off the baton of discipleship to the next generation. We have an internship program, and we have a hundred interns. I've been told, "We want the next generation to be bigger, stronger, and better than we are." Mark, our executive pastor, has really helped me in my role as strategy specialist here. He has seen my potential for the role that he currently has and has taken me under his wing, working with him. I am helping with driving and implementation and decision-making. I help with the innovation that happens, as well as buy-in. I help Mark run different departmental Intentional Growth Plans.

Mark brought me on because he saw my discontent that we would start something and not always stay the course. Now we are better at staying on course. I was walking by an office where an intern was working with a photography team. He was using the Four Helpful Lists, doing his own assessment! It is really cool seeing the tools being kept in front of people.

How has this happened? We have realigned our fiscal calendar to have movement in the same direction. In January, we run an overall Intentional Growth Plan. In February, we run departmental IGPs. In March, we take the information and start building a budget for the coming year. We set up our VIP teams to begin then as well. Come April, we take our overall budget that has been informed by our whole church and specific departments. Now we have some real numbers. That goes to our directors / board of elders. We get a ratification on the top number. They say yes or we have to massage it.

In April, we build an on-ramp to our All-In Campaign. Around here we go "all in" with our time, talent, and treasure. Every year we ask our people, "What next step does God want us to take?" All of that is informed by the IGP. We have a three-week on-ramp and then a big-gift Sunday. Will we be able to do this? In June, we do a little more on-ramp work. Then, in July, we go live!

For more stories and case studies, please visit www.intentionalchurches.com.

ACKNOWLEDGMENTS

I (Doug) would like to thank Dale Harlow for believing in a young kid far from God. You showed me Jesus and why a focus on the ONE can change a family tree. Thanks to Dick Hess (and Jenanne!) for challenging me to lead and acting as if I knew what I was doing at twenty years old. Thank you, Kevin Odor, for focusing on my emotional health. I am still in ministry because of your leadership. Finally, thanks to my beautiful and entrepreneurial wife, Jennifer, and my daughters for empowering me to go for it *always*! Anything is possible with God.

I (Bart) would like to thank Catherine, Luke, and Lila for believing in me, Intentional Churches, and this project. Your many prayers have mattered, and your faith inspires me every day. Dad and Mom (Wally and Barbara), hopefully you see your DNA as followers and leaders in this book. You taught me to love Jesus, love his bride, and chase the ONE. Thank you for leading churches that care about double kingdom impact and are built to make Jesus famous. Glen Schneider, Mike Bodine, Jud Wilhite, and Gene Appel, you are truly leaders of leaders. I can't thank you enough for what I've learned from you while serving at Crossroads and Central.

We (Doug and Bart) would like to thank the Intentional Churches team of coaches and facilitators. Your friendship is a constant source of encouragement to us. You are brothers and sisters and personal friends and mentors. We couldn't have written this book without you. Your decades of church leadership insights have been poured into this book. We pray we did them justice. We can't imagine doing ministry without you.

Thank you to the Intentional Churches staff team: Tasha Johnson, Kristi Andrade, Lynda Rec, Ashlea Kurcz, Jan Greggo, and Tyler Feller. You have shown much courage and patience alongside us. There is no way we would be here as serving church leaders without you. You embody our core values of putting the church first and five-star service. Your heart, passion, and attention to detail matter to us. They also matter to the many church leaders we serve each year. You honor God with your steadfast faith in his bride, and many people have been reached and will yet be reached because of you.

This project would not have happened without the detailed eyes and minds of Krista Petty and Chris Colvin. Thank you for your editing, writing, insights, restructuring, thoughts, and opinions alongside a couple of guys who are anything but authors. To the many other editors, we also say thank you. You had no small task!

Thanks to Greg Ligon, Kadi Cole, and our growing network of friends at Leadership Network. Thanks for your faith in us and your willingness to partner. We can't wait to do more ministry together while we listen, innovate, curate, and collaborate in his name. Joey Paul, thanks to you and the folks at Harper for joining us in impacting the kingdom through the local church.

We stand on the shoulders of too many leaders to list. Doug Slaybaugh, your friendship, encouragement, and discernment are unparalleled. You are one of a kind. Because of you, we have been directly impacted by Pete Richardson and Tom Paterson, whose thumbprints are on all of us.

Finally, thanks to the many leaders who have trusted us to work with your team. We know what it means to let us do so. It takes great courage, humility, and conviction to jump into something like ChurchOS and give it your all. We are humbled every time. You are our heroes. (We mean it!) You are our extended church leadership family, and we can't wait to stand together in heaven, swap stories, and celebrate the eternal ripple effect of your ministries.

To reach the ONE, in his name, only for his glory.

ABOUT INTENTIONAL CHURCHES

Intentional Churches exists to build a movement of churches that consistently activate the Great Commission: making more and better disciples. We have built an operating system called ChurchOS based on the timeless truths of Scripture to help the local church become strong and resilient. It includes a Living Toolbox, Intentional Growth Planning, and the Great Commission Engine, which create powerful, repeatable, and practical church leadership conversations and plans. It eliminates the hunger for silver-bullet solutions and creates confidence in the leaders who use it.

We support ChurchOS with coaching and training for leaders with a passion to reach the lost and deepen the saved. We offer options to begin the ChurchOS and Intentional Church journey. This often begins with an Intentional Growth Plan that includes a two-day install of the Living Toolbox, along with VIPs, immediate action, and a full year with an IC coach for training, resources, and accountability. Contact us or visit our website to learn more (https://intentional-churches.com). Church leaders are our heroes, and we hope you'll join the movement soon.

OUR DREAM FOR ChurchOS

SYNERGY

Imagine hundreds or thousands of churches using the same underlying processes to create a common platform for leadership and execution. This generates the ability to collaborate and discover new and improved approaches at a rapid rate, more rapid than ever before.

TIMELINESS

The software developers (aka strategy and program developers) create church-smart solutions with an understanding of how the church was meant to work. These solutions are not silver bullets but rather smart bullets designed to accomplish the church's mission in today's context. The software is a means to an end, not the end in itself.

REPEATABILITY

The rhythms and routines involved in an OS create unparalleled gains in effort and efficiency, allowing leaders to dedicate the resulting new energy to going deeper and wider on the best solutions for our churches and our communities. The Great Commission impact is greater than ever before.

ADAPTABILITY

As times change, technology develops, and the tribe of growing churches produces new ideas. With a standard operating system, the church can apply these solutions at the right time in the most effective way. Imagine churches as some of the most adaptable organizations on the planet when driven by the power and insight of the Holy Spirit.

PREDICTABILITY

No longer do churches wonder if our solutions are going to work or not. The crowdsourcing of the right solutions and smart development, combined with a deep understanding of the underlying dynamics, allow leaders to predict the result of applying new solutions and strategies. This greatly reduces the guesswork in church leadership.

ALIGNMENT

An OS allows teams and departments to operate in a similar way. Common understanding and a shared language are created. Ministry leaders are on the same page at all times, helping one another be more effective regardless of their roles.

SIMPLICITY

One of the greatest advancements of the modern operating system is the graphical user interface (GUI). Graphics allow you to intuitively understand how software is supposed to interact with hardware. But what's more important, graphics help you simply understand how to use the software to the greatest benefit! Imagine such simplicity being applied to your daily church leadership.

CONFIDENCE

Great operating systems just work. You turn on the power, boot up the software, and you are ready to go. You don't question the mechanics. You just create the right inputs and the results flow. We need this when it comes to the Great Commission. Imagine no more questions or fear that might slow us down or derail our efforts.

We can't wait to meet you soon.

ADDITIONAL RESOURCES

H ere are some books that have helped us along the way. We hope they will help you as well.

Bossidy, Larry, and Ram Charan. *Execution: The Discipline of Getting Things Done.* New York: Crown Business, 2002.

Ellis, Joe S. *The Church on Purpose: Keys to Effective Church Leadership.* Cincinnati: Standard, 1982.

George, Carl. *How to Break Growth Barriers: Capturing Overlooked Opportunities for Church Growth.* Grand Rapids: Baker, 1993.

McChesney, Chris, Sean Covey, and Jim Huling. *The Four Disciplines of Execution: Achieving Your Wildly Important Goals.* New York: Free Press, 2012.

McGavran, Donald A., and Winfield C. Arn. *Ten Steps for Church Growth.* San Francisco: Harper & Row, 1977.

McIntosh, Gary. *Taking Your Church to the Next Level: What Got You Here Won't Get You There.* Grand Rapids: Baker Books, 2009.

———, and Charles Arn. *What Every Pastor Should Know: 101 Indispensable Rules of Thumb for Leading Your Church.* Grand Rapids: Baker Books, 2013.

Malphurs, Aubrey. *Advanced Strategic Planning: A 21st-Century Model for Church and Ministry Leaders.* 3rd edition. Grand Rapids: Baker Books, 2013.

Mancini, Will. *Church Unique: How Missional Leaders Cast Vision, Capture Culture, and Create Movement.* San Francisco: Jossey-Bass, 2008.

Paterson, Tom. *Living the Life You Were Meant to Live.* Nashville: Thomas Nelson, 1998.

Rainer, Thom S., and Eric Geiger. *Simple Church: Returning to God's Process for Making Disciples.* Nashville: Broadman, 2006.

Russell, Bob. *When God Builds a Church: Ten Principles for Growing a Dynamic Church—The Remarkable Story of Southeast Christian Church.* West Monroe, LA: Howard, 2000.

Stanley, Andy. *Deep and Wide: Creating Churches Unchurched People Love to Attend.* Grand Rapids: Zondervan, 2012.

———. *Visioneering.* Colorado Springs: Multnomah, 1999.

———, Reggie Joiner, and Lane Jones. *Seven Practices of Effective Ministry.* Sisters, OR: Multnomah, 2004.

Waltz, Mark L. *Lasting Impressions: From Visiting to Belonging.* Loveland, CO: Group, 2009.

Warren, Rick. *The Purpose Driven Church: Growth Without Compromising Your Message and Mission.* Grand Rapids: Zondervan, 1995.

NOTES

INTRODUCTION

1. Todd Wilson and Dave Ferguson, *Becoming a Level Five Multiplying Church Field Guide* (EX Publishing, 2015), 32.
2. *The Great Opportunity: The American Church in 2050*, Pinetops Foundation White Paper 2017.

CHAPTER 1: THE INTENTIONAL LEADER

1. Thomas Paterson and Pete Richardson, *StratOp for Churches: The Art of Facilitating Strategic Operating Plans for Church* (Paterson Center LLC, 2017), 15.
2. John Kim, "Jeff Bezoz: 'All Overnight Success Takes About 10 Years'," *Consultant's Mind* (blog), May 19, 2018, https://www.consultantsmind .com/2018/05/19/jeff-bezos-all-overnight-success-takes-about-10-years/.

CHAPTER 3: THE GREAT COMMISSION ENGINE (PART 1)

1. [info to come]

CHAPTER 4: THE GREAT COMMISSION ENGINE (PART 2)

1. Rick Warren, *The Purpose Driven Life* (Grand Rapids: Zondervan, 2002), 17.
2. Gary L. McIntosh and Charles Arn, *What Every Pastor Should Know: 101 Indispensable Rules of Thumb for Leading Your Church* (Barker Books, 2013), 73–74.

CHAPTER 5: SQUATTERS, CUL-DE-SACS, AND BUFFETS

1. Wikipedia, "Engel Scale," last edited June 28, 2019, https://en.wikipedia.org/wiki/Engel_scale.
2. Greg L. Hawkins and Cally Parkinson, *Move: What 1,000 Churches Reveal About Spiritual Growth* (Grand Rapids: Zondervan, 2011).
3. Andy Stanley, Reggie Joiner, and Lane Jones, *7 Practices of Effective Ministry* (Sisters, OR: Multnomah, 2004).
4. Barna Group, *Reviving Evangelism: Current Realities That Demand a New Vision for Sharing Faith* (Ventura, CA: Barna Resources, 2019).
5. Chip and Dan Heath, *The Power of Moments: Why Certain Experiences Have Extraordinary Impact* (New York: Simon & Schuster, 2017).

CHAPTER 6: WHO IS YOUR ONE?

1. Bill W., *Alcoholics Anonymous: The Story of How Many Thousands of Men and Women Have Recovered from Alcoholism* (New York: Alcoholics Anonymous World Services, 1939).

CHAPTER 8: DOUBLE VISION: THE TENSION OF TRUE NORTH

1. Bob Goff, *Love Does: Discover a Secretly Incredible Life in an Ordinary World* (Nashville: Thomas Nelson, 2012).

CHAPTER 9: VISIONARY DECISIONS

1. Anthony "Tony" Campolo, *It's Friday, but Sunday's Coming* (Waco, TX: Word, 1984).
2. Charles E. Hummel, *Freedom from Tyranny of the Urgent* (Downers Grove, IL: InterVarsity, 1997).

CHAPTER 10: GO AND GROW

1. "Little Boy and Fat Man," Atomic Heritage Foundation, July 23, 2014, https://www.atomicheritage.org/history/little-boy-and-fat-man.
2. Liz Wiseman and Gary McKeown, *Multipliers: How the Best Leaders Make Everyone Smarter* (New York: HarperBusiness, 2010), https://johnmattone.com/liz-wiseman-on-important-leadership-lessons-for-john-mattone/.
3. Jim Collins and Morten T. Hansen, *Great by Choice: Uncertainty, Chaos, and Luck—Why Some Thrive Despite Them All* (New York: HarperCollins, 2011).

ABOUT THE AUTHORS

BART RENDEL, cofounder and president, Intentional Churches: Bart has dedicated his life to helping churches reach more people for Christ. His passion for serving churches comes from his upbringing as a pastor's kid and learning from his parents about the intentionality of reaching and growing people in Christ. His conviction runs deep. Bart served as an executive leader for over eighteen years at Crossroads Christian Church in Lexington, Kentucky, and Central Christian Church in Las Vegas, Nevada, where he and his family remain deeply connected. He and his wife, Catherine, have two children. Bart occasionally plays a round of golf, but he always takes in Kentucky Wildcats games.

DOUG PARKS, cofounder and CEO, Intentional Churches: Doug's love and commitment to help churches comes from his own experience of being eternally impacted as a teenager by a committed church leader. He served for seventeen years as the executive pastor at Canyon Ridge Christian Church in Las Vegas, Nevada. Prior to Canyon Ridge, Doug was a Chick-fil-A owner/operator in Cincinnati, Ohio, where he won the coveted Symbol of Success award. Doug and his wife, Jennifer, reside in Las Vegas with their two children, but he still finds time to follow sports, including his beloved Ohio State Buckeyes.